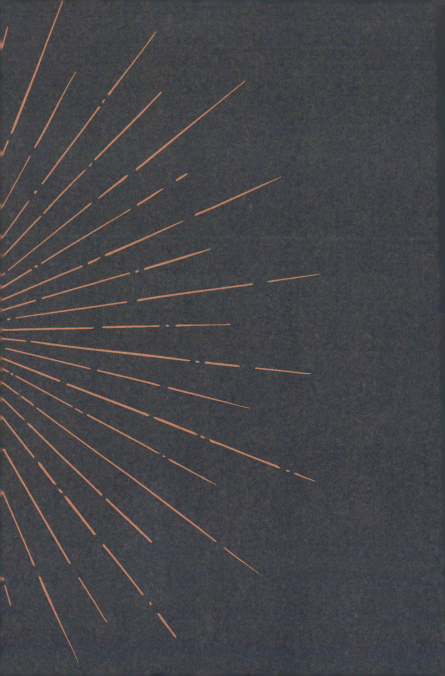

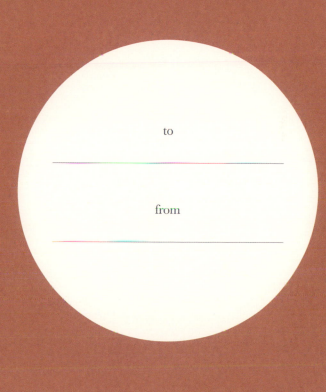

to

_____

from

_____

Radiate: 90 Devotions to Reflect the Heart of Jesus
Copyright © Cleere Cherry Reaves. All rights reserved.
First Edition, August 2021

Published by:

21154 Highway 16 E
Siloam Springs, AR 72761
dayspring.com

Written by: Cleere Cherry Reaves
Cover Design: Lauren Purtle

Printed in China
Prime: J6788
ISBN: 978-1-64870-290-7

RADIATE

Contents

LETTER TO READER

Hi, friend!

It's Cleere. Man do I wish I could be talking to you in person and thanking you for opening the pages of this devotional. Do you know how excited I am that you're here? And engaged in your life and what God wants for you?

Writing this devotional really challenged my heart. I was continually humbled by the fact that He would use me—someone who is flawed and, trust me, far from perfect—to write a devotional about how to shine His light. Despite ourselves, He loves nothing more than to partner with His children to shake the world. It reminded me that He doesn't need my performance or for me to impress Him; nor does He desire for me to leave the mess before approaching His throne. He longs for me to bring all that I am and lay it at His feet. Then, as I sit in His presence and seek shelter under the shadow of His wings, learning His heart as I receive His unfailing love, I become emboldened and empowered to live in a way that reflects Him.

This is my hope for you and me—we are in this together.

May we be the people who stop and listen to the stories of those around us, showing His gentleness.

May we be the people who give without fearing scarcity, displaying His generosity.

May we be the people who speak life and walk in faith no matter the circumstances, revealing His peace.

May we be the people who offer help regardless of reciprocation and show up well for others, pointing to His kindness.

May we radiate His heart on the mountaintop, in the valley, and amid our everyday moments.

I hope this devotional meets you right where you are, encourages your heart, and propels you forward as you lock arms with Jesus.

Let's get after it. This broken world around us needs exactly what we have.

Let's radiate.

Xoxo,
Cleere

You are the light of the world—like a
city on a hilltop that cannot be hidden.
MATTHEW 5:14 NLT

P.S. If you want to follow me for daily encouragement,
find me @cleerelystated on Instagram + Facebook!
Would love to see you there.

Childlike Faith

See that you do not despise one of these little ones. For I tell you that in heaven their angels always see the face of my Father who is in heaven.

MATTHEW 18:10 ESV

Have you ever noticed how children don't worry about what they will eat, wear, or have tomorrow? They walk in the door from playing outside and immediately blurt out, "Mom, I'm hungry. What's for dinner?" They are fully confident, expecting there is already a plan and provision for them to eat. They fall asleep in their mother's arms at night knowing that when they rise in the morning, they will be safely in their beds, covered, cared for, and perfectly okay.

We claim that children don't worry as much because they have not been exposed to the real world like adults; we assume this should fade once maturity sets in and life reveals its less romantic side, right? However, what if spiritual maturity is much closer to a child's faith than we realize, with confident expectation of what is to come? This ability to live in the present, fully trusting the One whom they belong to, allows them to radiate joy and purity like we have never seen! Children are dependent on their parents with no shame in that dependence. They do not wonder if they will be provided for or loved; their assumption is that they will continue to receive what they have always been given. Children forgive quickly and love even quicker because they operate on the basis of being loved.

God desperately wants us, His children, to operate in this same confidence in His character. His steady faithfulness and care for our future allows us to live in the present. The childlike faith that we once displayed is not because we were unaware; it's because we blindly trusted in our caretaker for what was to come. Such purity is to be preserved and protected and serves as a reminder for us all. People who know that they are loved radiate the love of Jesus in return. Their worry lines are replaced with laugh lines as they anchor themselves in Jesus.

Haven't we seen that God is far more pleased with our trusting in Him than He is impressed with our knowledge of Him? The trust is the application of believing the knowledge is true. Like a child, may we run and play and trust our Father will provide.

Prayer

Hey Jesus, thank You for the innocence, purity, and trust of a childlike faith. Help me see my heavenly Father correctly—as faithful, good, and loving. Today I choose to freely play and be, knowing You will provide all that I need in due time. In Jesus' name,

AMEN.

Hospitality like No Other

Share with the LORD's people who
are in need. Practice hospitality.

ROMANS 12:13 NIV

We walked in and saw the table was set. There
were notes on each of our plates, carefully
placed for each of us. Chicken salad croissants,
our favorite homemade dip, and a key lime pie
were prepared for us to devour. She knew we
would be hungry when we walked in, even though
we weren't aware of our hunger until we smelled the
food. I knew she had her own set of to-dos that day, but
she chose to serve us, and in doing so, she ministered to us in
a way we were not expecting.

As we sat and devoured our lunch, she asked questions about our day, what
we were enjoying these days, and what Jesus was doing in our lives. Her
genuine curiosity and desire to converse with us made us feel special and
seen, as if the homemade lunch wasn't enough on its own.

Hospitality is often described and imagined in tangible ways—the food
that is prepared, the table that is set, and the service that is extended. However, the enjoyment of the receiver is found in the spirit of the giver, not
the gift. The lunch experience I described above is one I will never forget not because of the delicious food but because of the thoughtfulness
that carried it. This lovely lady had no obligation to feed us; she received
no payment for doing so—in fact, she spent her own money, offered her
own atmosphere, gave her own time, and sacrificed her own schedule to
be present for ours. And the craziest part? She thanked us—like, she was

genuinely grateful—for our presence and our consuming of what she had made.

This living sermon opened my eyes even wider to the hospitality of our heavenly Father. He isn't rushed; He gives us His attention. He knows our needs before we know them, and He considers it a joy to meet them. He thinks of our most favorite things and smiles as He prepares them for us to enjoy. He delights in our delight because He knows it will lead us to His feet. He cares about the depth of our souls—our worries, big and small, and the greatest hopes in our hearts. He wants to hear it all. As we sit at His table and enjoy the gifts and presence of our King, our lives are marked by such hospitality and care. What did we do to deserve a life so sweet?

May our hands be willing to give to others the same treatment of grace we have been extended. Whether it be through intentional conversation, a heartfelt prayer, or a "welcome to the neighborhood" chocolate pie, we can radiate the care of Jesus in any space we find ourselves—what an opportunity!

Prayer

Dear Jesus, thank You for the table You set before me. You give me all that I need and far more than I could ever deserve. Help me to offer that same care and concern for others. In Jesus' name,

AMEN.

Refined Radiance

We all, with unveiled face, beholding the glory of the LORD, are being transformed into the same image from one degree of glory to another. For this comes from the LORD who is the Spirit.

II CORINTHIANS 3:18 ESV

It's been said that when they asked Michelangelo how he created the sculpture of David, he said he simply chiseled away what wasn't David. His vision of David's true stature and makeup was always there; he just had to remove what stood in the way. Thinking about this is mind-boggling. How is it possible to have such vision and clarity of what is not yet there? Or, rather, the discernment and care to remove what shouldn't be?

The same is true of us with Jesus. He is chiseling away at everything that doesn't look like Him. This refinement process is often hard because the extra allows us to hide. It keeps us covered in what we believe is self-protection. However, our Father knows it is just the opposite. And so He chisels, cleanses, corrects, disciplines, and fine-tunes us. All of this is grace even when it doesn't feel like grace; it is the unveiling of the promised and the possible because He sees what we cannot.

May we give Him our timelines and our treasures, certain that His riches are better than gold. We do not need to fear the unknown or impossible, as He can do any and all things. May we offer Him our dreams and our hopes, assured that His plans for us are far better than life could offer. May we hand over the desire for perfection, the pressure to conform, and the temptation to compare, fully confident that He is the author of everything beautiful, good, and sure.

This is just it—the answer, the solution, the plan, the point. We need to give it all up. To lay it down. All the bricks, just take them all out. Isn't it so crazy that we work so hard to hold what's heavy when we have the divine ability to take it off and travel lightly? And in relinquishing all, He makes us whole. Complete. Continually working out what must go so that only He can remain.

Each of us is David, as we are continually being transformed through what is stripped away. We are refined so that we may radiate a God so good, a grace so sweet.

Prayer

Hey Jesus, thank You for Your continual care to chisel away what must go. Remind me that whatever You take is for my best; I can trust Your vision with all that I have and all that I am. In Jesus' name,

AMEN.

The Narrow Way

The LORD will establish you as a holy
people to himself, as he has sworn to
you, if you keep the commandments of
the LORD your God and walk in his ways.

DEUTERONOMY 28:9 ESV

There's a path we tend to travel down—it's the
one we have grown accustomed to. The one of
least resistance. We don't even mean to choose it;
it's just what we have always chosen.

Our habits and tendencies are based on the truth we've
rehearsed in our heads. We find ourselves reacting in auto-
mation, making us robotic instead of responsive. Because we
know the turns of this path, we set out for it, pack our desired lunch,
and move ahead, looking forward to the view that we know lies before
us—that is, until we realize that the road ahead becomes stagnant and easy.
Our growth and strength are no longer required to walk this path, so we
begin to desire a new way.

But we also know this new path will require much processing before pleasure. It will force us to pull out some tools that have gotten rusty and put
our hands in the dirt. The rain has fallen on the roots in this space, and
they've anchored themselves deep into the soil of our lives. And as much as
we would like to avoid the hard stuff, we also know it's the heart stuff. The
hard place to get our heart healthy. The path with great resistance that will
yield a strong soul. It will produce the fruit that makes for a life worth living.

But as we show up in this new space, afraid it will be too much, we stop worrying about the rich view and we commit to the process of where we stand. It may not seem beautiful at first glance, but it ushers in a dependence, a breaking, an honesty that we weren't experiencing along our familiar ways. We feel the sweat drip down our face and hit the soil, and we hear our heavenly Father speak over us, "I see you and I'm proud. Stay the course."

Life. We get to make the decision over and over again—will we choose what is already available and close or will we choose the riches only found by digging in the dirt? Will we be brave? We decide every day, in many capacities and in many ways. And the more that we pick the hard but the healthy and the holy, the more we understand that DEEP joy is often the result of difficulty + dependence. Leaning in, listening intently, and learning about the differences between heaven and earth and how we live in the in-between. Radiating from Jesus is the light that is worth sifting through all the darkness.

Prayer

Hey Jesus, thank You for Your patience with my heart. When comfort is tempting, realign me with truth. Help me desire the narrow way and live my life according to Your Word. In Jesus' name,

AMEN.

Vulnerability Connects Us

He said to me, "My grace is sufficient for you, for my power is made perfect in weakness." Therefore I will boast all the more gladly of my weaknesses, so that the power of Christ may rest upon me.

II CORINTHIANS 12:9 ESV

Isn't it interesting how when we are around other people who are transparent and courageous in what they share, we find it inspiring and warm, yet when it is us, we feel like our vulnerability can quickly become a sign of weakness or incompetence?

Our stories are our personal way of sharing the brilliance of human frailty when interceded by the unlimited, unwavering power of a sovereign God. When we open our hearts up to others and allow them to know us, we are offering an invitation for they themselves to be known. While it may be our abilities and gifts that temporarily impress others, it is our vulnerability and struggles that connect us.

All of us desire to be loved for who we truly are, but how can someone love us in our mess if they aren't even aware of it? If we reserve our friendships for our highlight reel and we don't invite others into the trenches, we cannot blame loneliness in the battle. Jesus wants us to fight for each other, but that requires being both the one who is willing to listen and the one who is willing to share. Even greater than our relationships on this earth, our vulnerability radiates our ultimate trust in and dependence on Jesus. When we are forthright in our imperfections but still carrying on in peace and connection, it shows that we have found our confidence in a far deeper, richer place—at His feet.

Radiating Jesus does not resemble someone who "has it all together"; radiating Jesus looks like someone who has chosen to commit themselves to reflecting the truth that *He* holds it all together. He created us with the desire to be known by Him and loved by Him. When we hide ourselves in Him, we will no longer feel the pressure to hide ourselves from others. He becomes our refuge to radiate to a world that is in desperate need of Christ-like community.

Prayer

Hey Jesus, thank You for meeting me directly in my mess and transforming me from the inside out. Help me to be vulnerable with others and trust in You for my protection. Authentic friendship requires that we open ourselves up and know You cover us. In Jesus' name,

AMEN.

Radical Acceptance

Therefore welcome one another as Christ has welcomed you, for the glory of God.

ROMANS 15:7 ESV

Remember the story from Scripture about the woman who was bleeding for twelve years and touched the robe of Jesus? The story is recorded in the Gospel of Mark, and when we actually step back to imagine this story taking place in real time, it's awe-inspiring.

A woman who was deeply familiar with suffering but had great faith, she believed that if she could touch the hem of Jesus' robe, that alone would have the power to completely restore her health. And it did! What must Jesus have radiated to exude that kind of power? How would a woman who had been rejected by so many around her feel comfortable enough to do such a thing? It is because our King Jesus never walked a step without humility. He radiated absolute acceptance regardless of socioeconomic status, physical appearance, workplace performance, or cultural background. There were no prequalifications for His love. In fact, He was drawn to the lost, the hurting, the rejected, and the sinner. That's why He came. He sat with the tax collectors, healed the blind, restored the purity of prostitutes, and welcomed the forgotten. This kind of reputation builds a foundation for true unity—all may come.

If we are desiring to radiate the same acceptance as our Savior, we will never achieve it by staying in our comfort zones or surrounding ourselves with those who are similar to us. Familiarity is a dangerous covering when it becomes our reason for not extending a hand or lending ourselves to another.

What would it look like to radiate acceptance in our lives? It's as simple as choosing a different way to congregate at the pool, changing our conversations with friends, inviting another to lunch, or reframing our mental dialogue to accept rather than judge. If the King of perfection determined His standards were all-inclusive, shouldn't we?

This does not mean we don't establish boundaries. Our acceptance of another does not automatically condone their lifestyle or choices. However, if we choose to reject others rather than love them, our impact becomes impossible because our proximity is nonexistent. We cannot give light and love to those we exclude.

May we do our own heart check and ask Him: "Can You reveal to me any way I've made my love seem exclusive to others? Open my eyes and my heart—I want to accept and love like You do."

Prayer

Hey Jesus, thank You for Your unending grace and kindness that accepts me just as I am. Help me to give this kind of radical acceptance to others, offering them a safe place to land and a secure friend. Show me how to have a long table and an open door to all. In Jesus' name,

AMEN.

His Presence Perfects

I will put this third into the fire, and refine them
as one refines silver, and test them as gold is
tested. They will call upon my name, and I will
answer them. I will say, "They are my people";
and they will say, "The LORD is my God."

ZECHARIAH 13:9 ESV

Many of us hear the word *radiate* and our minds
correlate it with appearance. What we imagine is
something that emits light that is noticeable from the
outside. As members of the human race, we assume
that this route to radiance is achieved through perfecting
our own image. Whether it be through Instagram, the cultural standard, or how we compare to others, we tend to feel the
weight of our imperfections is too great to bear. But Jesus has never
asked nor desired for us to "clean ourselves up" and then present our lives
to Him! It has always been that as we spend time in His presence, studying
His perfection and His image, He refines us from the inside out.

Unfortunately, radiance is not an outside job. The only part we play in the
purification of our own hearts is placing ourselves at His feet. There, we
learn the heartbeat of our Father, the ways of His hands, and the glory of
His face. And in turn, we begin to look like Him. Psalm 139 reminds us
that He crafted us in His image. As we receive greater revelation of this
truth, our souls begin to shine. The weight of perfection now removed
from our shoulders, we start to prioritize the desires of our heavenly Father.

We must ask ourselves, What good is all our "doing" if it is redecorating a
house that has a weak foundation? If our inner workings are not built on
Him, our functionality becomes futile and our future is compromised. The

permanence and power of a place is ultimately determined by its foundation, not its presentation. When the storms come and life brings the rain, true confidence and hope are found deep below the surface.

Our hearts were created to pursue beauty—that in and of itself is not a bad thing. However, when we attempt to find lasting fulfillment through impressing others with the outside, we will always leave disappointed.

The King is perfecting us. As we sit with Him and let ourselves be loved, His presence refines us. Let's let the waves refine us as we rest in the Creator and Calmer of the seas.

Prayer

Hey Jesus, thank You for the way You are continually refining my heart. Though uncomfortable and sometimes painful, I know it is where life is found. Remind me to see Your correction as kindness and Your purification as grace. In Jesus' name,

AMEN.

Silence Ushers In Light

My soul, wait in silence for God alone, for my
hope is from Him. He alone is my rock and my
salvation, my refuge; I will not be shaken.

PSALM 62:5–6 NASB

Silence tends to scare us. Despite our pleas for
quiet and our desperation to hear God, we often
reach for some kind of noise to fill the airwaves.
Whether through podcasts, music, phone calls, or
Netflix, we feel the silence approaching and fear loneliness will be accompanying it. Silence would require
us to be alone with our thoughts, and the things we have
been avoiding or anxious about would have to surface.

However, this quiet can be our best friend. It allows us to slow down
the avalanche of anxiety and deal with the root of how our mind arrived
at this place. Turning down the volume of all the voices that surround us
gives us the capability to turn up the affirmation, guidance, and clarity of
our Savior. We usually don't even realize how loud our lives are until we
experience the luxury of stillness. Just being with Jesus. Sitting, listening,
leaning in to drink from His well and discover His heart. It is this time with
Him that gives us the wisdom to speak into the lives of others and have
direction for our own future. It is this discipline of being at His feet that
helps us prioritize what is important and establish healthy rhythms for all
areas of our lives, not just the spiritual.

Radiance is the result of developing an inner sanctuary. This deep attitude
of the heart is not merely a place but a posture that becomes portable with
every step we take. Outwardly, we may be tending to our everyday, mundane tasks, but inwardly we can be praying, talking to Jesus, or worshiping

in song and dance. The countenance of our soul becomes pleasant and fulfilled as we delight ourselves in Him.

And how do we cultivate this inner sanctuary? By quieting the noise, clearing the clutter, and sitting at the feet of our heavenly Father. We do not have to be loud for our souls to speak loudly of Jesus. As we discipline ourselves to listen to truth, His promises will radiate hope into our lives. And this hope will provide the sacred space we were longing for—to be a people who remain a light in the darkness and hold tightly to the love of an everlasting Father.

Prayer

Hey Jesus, thank You for reminding me that silence is not the absence of You but rather the space where I can finally hear You speak. Show me how to cultivate this inner sanctuary and develop a posture of peace, regardless of my circumstances. In Jesus' name,

AMEN.

The Fruitful Life

> But the fruit of the Spirit is love, joy,
> peace, forbearance, kindness, goodness,
> faithfulness, gentleness and self control.
> Against such things there is no law.
>
> GALATIANS 5:22–23 NIV

Love, joy, peace, patience, kindness, goodness, faithfulness, gentleness, and self-control. The fruit of the Spirit is the true recipe for reflecting the heart of our Maker. But . . . how do we get there?

We all have probably enjoyed a juicy peach or a fresh strawberry. Its taste is so rich in flavor—delicious and healthy all at the same moment. But this fruit that we savor is only cultivated through the soil of hard work and the art of intention. What we come to enjoy is only possible because of another's dedicated labor and care.

While not physical, it is the same with the fruit of the Spirit. Through the study of the Word, we learn how to extend kindness to our neighbor. Digging into the truth of Jesus reminds us that we are to love one another as He loves us.

Our patience while waiting on a promise is cultivated through learning to trust our Jesus. What felt like a delay becomes an opportunity as we discover that God's timing and awareness are always perfect.

As we pray and seek Jesus, patience and gentleness make themselves known. Sitting with the Savior has a way of revealing to us any hardness that we have and the need to let Him soften it. He helps us remember the patience we ourselves have been extended, and in doing so, our hearts are more able to be gentle with others.

Many desire the outcomes of working hard but will spend their lives trying to find a shortcut. The path to holiness does not require perfection; rather, it asks that we bring all our imperfections into the care of the King—the ultimate Farmer. Fruit has its seasons. There will be times in our lives when we'll need to pursue peace. Other times, we will feel the significance of exerting self-control. But these fruits are both circular and all-inclusive. Through our righteousness in Jesus, if we have access to one, we have access to all. No matter your personality type or love language, all are at your disposal.

They also support one another; as we learn to operate in gentleness, the fruit of joy is sweetly on our lips. By grace, the Lord helps us experience and tap into what we could never experience on our own. He is not asking us to pursue every fruit at all moments—such usually results in performance-based faith (aka striving). Rather, it is simply in our pursuit of Him that we find all the fruits on the table as we gather with Him. Radiantly on display, He tells us, "Take and receive."

Prayer

Hey Jesus, thank You for giving me full and forever access to the fruit of the Spirit. Help me to tap into it, leaning on Your strength inside of me and not my own. As I gather at Your table, You provide all that I need. In Jesus' name,

AMEN.

Returning to Him

God is able to make all grace abound to you, so that having all sufficiency in all things at all times, you may abound in every good work.

II CORINTHIANS 9:8 ESV

There are many ways in which we enjoy the sun and come to know its light. Some days it gives us adventure as it shines on the sand beneath our feet and makes for the perfect beach vacation. Other days, its rays are the warmth that makes our cold bodies keep moving. The sun embodies fresh mercy as it rises again in the morning and is the posture of consistency as it sets at night. And when the rains come and the sun reappears, it whispers to our soul, "This too shall pass."

The sun doesn't change, but what it offers us is based on what we need in that moment. Our perception of its light is through the filter of what we are already searching for. It is much the same in the way that Jesus radiates through us. We do not need to worry about being all things to all people; we simply saturate ourselves in His Word and His love, and He will grace us with what we need to give others. That is the beauty of being hidden in Him.

One day, we might be delivering food to a family in need, personifying how God supplies and equips us. Another day, it might just be praying with a friend and reminding them of truth. This seemingly small response has the power to move the heavens and points to the intimate nature of God. And then some days, we might be taking a really big step or making a bold decision for our lives. This radical obedience and trust in His plan communicate to others the trust we have in God's voice.

And though we don't prefer this way, some days it will be us walking through the fire and still praising His name that will be our story. Such actions scream of the power of God—our struggles reminding others that His strength is most seen in our weakness.

The sun does not continually ask, "How must I alter myself to be of use?" Similarly, we must trust that when we turn to Jesus, He knows what the watching world needs and He can provide that for us. Let our striving cease and our surrendering remain, much like the sun—always itself but used by the Father in a million different ways.

Prayer

Hey Jesus, thank You for always helping me be what I need to be to those You want me to serve. Help me remember my value is not in striving but in simply following where You lead. You will bring the light when I open myself to You. In Jesus' name,

AMEN.

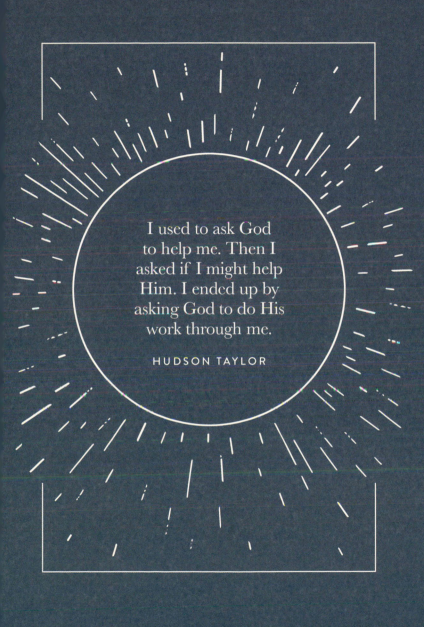

I used to ask God to help me. Then I asked if I might help Him. I ended up by asking God to do His work through me.

HUDSON TAYLOR

Excellence Wins

By His divine power, God has given us everything we need for living a godly life. We have received all of this by coming to know Him, the one who called us to Himself by means of His marvelous glory and excellence.

II PETER 1:3 NLT

There she was, the lady I could hear singing from one hundred feet away in the airport terminal, bringing sunshine to my crazy whirlwind of a day. As we got closer to the store where she was working, I surveyed her restocking drinks, rearranging books, and working the cash register, all while singing to customers about the love of Jesus and the need for joy. Within five minutes, she easily turned ten people's day around, including mine. But what mesmerized me the most was she was not just a joyous employee in attitude, she was working circles around the other employees. She could have sat still and just coasted amid transactions, but it was obvious that she took her obligations seriously and herself lightly.

We eventually had a conversation, and I was heavily impacted by her work ethic and care for mere strangers. Her lanyard had Jesus written on it, in case anyone was wondering where her joy was found. Her excellence was such an example to anyone watching, no matter what profession they entertained or wherever they were headed next. She realized the opportunity she had to make a difference right where she was, and she refused to miss it. Valerie was her name. And come to find out, the minute I posted something about Mrs. Valerie in the Charlotte airport, I found that she has lots of raving fans and admirers from all over! Valerie was aware of what God could do with the gifts that she has in the exact place she was, but she also knew it was going to require her to show up with an attitude of excellence.

Whatever it is that we do, we have the capacity, responsibility, and opportunity to give our all and our best. Even when we feel underappreciated, we can be sure that Jesus never misses anything. Also, the minute we truly understand what we actually deserve and the grace we have been given, we will never expect anything. All will be a gift, and our response will be gratitude, excellence, and joy.

God's people should be the brightest, most willing, kindest, most generous people in the world. We know the importance of what is to come and that time is limited! Let's show up, wherever we are, with a smile like Valerie's and a deep-seated joy and commitment to excellence with each step we take. It will win every time.

Prayer

Hey Jesus, thank You for giving me the desire to work with excellence and joy. Show me how to be an example to others, working for You and not for people. Your hope is my reward. In Jesus' name,

AMEN.

Heaven on the Horizon

Yet God has made everything beautiful for its own time. He has planted eternity in the human heart, but even so, people cannot see the whole scope of God's work from beginning to end.

ECCLESIASTES 3:11 NLT

We know we are eternal beings. Covered in flesh and placed on this earth, we were meant to feel a little strange here. Our heavenly Father never wanted us to get comfortable here because He knows our security is only found in our forever home with Him. This is why He deep-wired into us the hope of heaven. Ecclesiastes 3:11 tells us that we were made with eternity in our hearts. In other words, we have always been just passing through this world.

Life is hard though. The curveballs and confusion can make us feel crazy, and sometimes we find ourselves praying for a break. An escape. Just a release of some kind, right? Our times of struggle and the reality we find ourselves in should push us not to hopelessness or fear but rather to hope and faith. When the waves crash, we must realign our focus on the Maker of the sea. When the future feels dim, we must remember He is the Light of the world. Our citizenship is in heaven, but while we live here, we are called to bring heaven to earth. If our confidence, hope, and kindness look no different from the world's, what are we communicating about heaven?

When our perspective is based simply on what we see, we have quite a limited view. As children of the King, we have the supernatural ability to see our situation from the throne of heaven. As we lift our eyes from the dirt and we remember the divine, we will radiate the peace of God.

We do not get the luxury of living in a bubble and becoming irrelevant here. After all, we wouldn't even find fulfillment there because we were created for relationship and to make a difference! It is our desire for heaven that propels us forward as we discover God's handiwork here. The waves still crash, but our joy is found in the refinement as we keep a heavenly perspective. Is there anything more powerful than watching someone praise Him in the storm? Such faith reveals that we know the end of the story: Heaven is on the horizon. This truth is the peace that guards our souls.

Prayer

Hey Jesus, thank You for the promise and peace that heaven brings. With eternity in my heart, I find courage and confidence to move forward. Keep my mind fixed on You, the author and perfecter of my faith. In Jesus' name,

AMEN.

Holy Confidence

The LORD your God is the one who goes with you to fight for you against your enemies to give you victory.

DEUTERONOMY 20:4 NIV

We all know the story of David and Goliath. A shepherd boy with no experience on the battlefield proved himself to be a warrior. As the Israelites feared for their lives while Goliath paraded around, David showed up with simply his stones, a slingshot, and the strength of God on his side.

We see in I Samuel 17 that David didn't hesitate to fight Goliath. He proclaimed victory before he entered battle despite the fact that he was not wearing armor and lacked a sword. As David came on the scene, it is obvious that he recognized the opportunity. He recollected how God had been preparing him for such a time as this. He had fought off lions and bears while protecting his sheep, so why would he be afraid now? David's confidence was fully in the Lord; he knew that the ordinary stones he had would be enough to defeat the enemy. His victory over Goliath shocked his own brothers and radiated a holy confidence that deeply reflected the faithfulness and power of God.

We hear this story and it seems hard to relate. We forget that we don't have to be physically on a battlefield to be fighting a war. Our Goliath is often disguised as fear of the unknown, addiction, temptation, gossip, or anything that keeps us from advancing forward. We think to ourselves, "Surely these stones aren't enough." And so we pray for more than we have or an escape from where we are in order to experience victory.

But our God wants us to show up on the battlefield anyway. He wants us to trust that the preparation we have received is sufficient and that He will cover any space that we lack. After all, isn't the gap between what we have and where He is asking us to step or surrender called faith?

With our body shaking and our knees a little wobbly, may we walk forward. And as He secures our victory, our holy confidence will grow and we will learn, once again, that He can use our stones and our surrender to ensure our success.

Prayer

Hey Jesus, thank You for the reminder that my confidence is based on You, not me. The stones in my pocket are sufficient to fight Goliath because Your power is made perfect in my weakness. Thank You for assuring me victory. In Jesus' name,

AMEN.

What Are We Mirroring?

**The one who says that he remains in Him
ought, himself also, walk just as He walked.**

1 JOHN 2:6 NASB

Have you noticed how a married couple almost
starts to look alike? If the couple were just two
people in a random lineup, it might not seem
so apparent, but the longer they are together, the
more obvious it seems. It is as though the more
time they spend together, the more they reflect pieces
of each other.

As elementary as it may seem, the only way that we can mirror the heart of our heavenly Father is if we spend time with Him.
We can learn all about His kindness or His grace or His mercy or His
forgiveness, but until we experience it firsthand, it's hard to make it personal. And much like in a husband and wife relationship, each one benefits
from the goodness of the other. When a husband shows undeserved grace
to his wife, she can't help but be affected by it. It marks her soul. And when
a wife displays patience or gentleness, her husband notices its warmth. As
the relationship deepens and intimacy grows, each one begins to desire
giving the love they have received.

While we as humans could never offer anything good to a perfect Savior
that we did not first receive from Him anyway, we are continually being
transformed to mirror His heart. Not out of striving or obligation, but
rather through our worship and admiration we long to portray just a morsel of the love and tenderness we have been extended.

Who doesn't want to look like Jesus? He is perfection and peace personified. However, we can live a long time desiring to resemble someone but never develop the discipline of learning what they are like.

Prayer is not so much a problem answer method; rather, it's just a conversation. As we lean in and witness the love of a giving Father, we return to the table once more. And then again and again and again. Digging into His Word turns from a last resort to a first stop. His guidance and instruction become the sweetness of our lives. Solitude is no longer a task or a suggestion but a luxury and a dream for our spirit. The thought of just being with Him becomes our greatest desire.

Time spent together. Just being with Him. No performance necessary. But in turn, we will receive the greatest outcome we could ever hope for: reflecting and radiating the Savior of the world.

Prayer

Hey Jesus, thank You for wanting to spend time with me. My heart leaps knowing You don't just love me but You like me. Help me to yearn for time with You so that I can better reflect all that You are. In Jesus' name,

AMEN.

Friend for Life

No longer do I call you servants, for the servant does not know what his master is doing; but I have called you friends, for all that I have heard from my Father I have made known to you.

JOHN 15:15 ESV

Growing up, we made instant friends on the playground. There was no handpicking for four square or dodgeball; we were surrounded by our teammates, and onward we went. Then high school and college came, and each brought their challenges. We learned about the pain of gossip and the power of popularity and finding our place. The more people we met, the more we learned that we all are in search of belonging. The same desire put us all on an equal playing field.

And then came adulthood and we thought, "Surely friendship gets easier than it used to be, right?" While there are no school uniforms or assigned seating, the real world offers no formulas for finding lasting friendship. As we work through our new routines and walk through transitions of all sorts—moving, marriage, career changes, struggles, and relational changes—we discover that we are all still searching for those we can confide in, lean on, and have in our corner for life. Isn't it helpful to know that you aren't alone in your loneliness or in your yearning for true friendship? It comforts me.

Thankfully for us, Jesus wired us for community and modeled all throughout Scripture what it looked like to truly be a friend. He was brave, kind, honest, selfless, and sacrificial. He forgave quickly, walked with others through brokenness, and prayed with full belief that His heavenly Father was listening.

When His disciples betrayed Him,
He remained the friend He wished He had.

When His hometown rejected Him,
He remained the friend He wished He had.

When His followers doubted Him,
He remained the friend He wished He had.

What if we did as Jesus did and we decided to be the friend we pray for instead of the friend we feel others deserve? Maybe on the path of intentionality and through the avenue of sacrifice, we will discover that in being such a friend, we meet new friends along the way. Instead of focusing on our loneliness, we let His affirmation, tenderness, and love fill the void.

People will disappoint us, but when we place our faith in Jesus, we are free to just enjoy friendship with others rather than seek our fulfillment from them.

A friend for life—that is Jesus for us. When we hold this close to our hearts and take time to meet with Him, we equip ourselves with the ability to be that same kind of friend to others.

Prayer

Hey Jesus, thank You for being my friend. You give and You give and You give, knowing I can't reciprocate such kindness or generosity. Thank You for being my safe place. Show me how to be a trustworthy and gracious friend to all along the way. In Jesus' name,

AMEN.

City on a Hill

You are the light of the world—like a city
on a hilltop that cannot be hidden.

MATTHEW 5:14 NLT

We know that Jesus is the Light of the world.
If He had not come to save us, we would never
experience goodness, and only darkness would
exist. Because of who He is and the fact that we
are His children, we are now considered the light
of the world. We have been entrusted with the same
life-changing, world-altering divine holiness that Jesus
exuded, and as the Gospel of Matthew mentions, this
light, or "city on a hilltop," cannot be hidden (Matthew 5:14).

Sometimes we reject the notion that we were created to shine. This is
usually because we reflect on our own mistakes and see the frailness of our
humanity and doubt whether we are worthy. However, because we are
children of the Creator of light, this light that we radiate is woven into the
core of our being. When a city is located on a hill, the landscape of its existence makes it stand out. Nature sets it apart. It is taller, closer to heaven,
and raised up because of where it was placed. If that city experiences brokenness, destruction, or disobedience, is it still on a hill? Yes!

The same is true of our identity in Christ. Living mercy and tangible grace
in motion—that is us. We may desire to hide from ourselves because of our
struggles, but we have been placed on higher ground. We may feel unseen
by God during hard seasons, but just as Matthew says, how could such a
place be hidden? Our confirmed identity as heirs of Christ offers us an
unshakable promise—to be light in the darkness. It is not our performance
that provides true light; it is our remaining in the steadfastness of God's

character that ensures it. The reality of being on a hill can be difficult and great because, well, we are on a hill. This means that we are exposed and seen at all moments. This is no mistake, as we are called to live in the light—giving air to our weaknesses because that is how a watching world sees the strength and faithfulness of God.

We are a city on a hill. No matter the past we have endured, the socioeconomic background we come from, or the current state of our affairs, God has not changed His mind about us. Set apart, raised up, and able to light up the whole world if we trust in Him.

Prayer

Hey Jesus, thank You for positioning and placing me on solid ground. I see You at work in my weaknesses as You fight for me. Remind me of my identity, a city on a hill, meant to shine light on the watching world. In Jesus' name,

AMEN.

Peace like a River

Have you ever been around someone who radiated peace? It was not that they talked about it; rather, they lived it. The world could be in total disarray around them—plans could be getting canceled, people could be upset, and preparations could be exhausting—but it's like they had made a decision to just trust God. The state of their soul—seen by the countenance on their face and the disposition of their spirit—is not flaky or fickle. It is a resting peace, a lasting peace, and it is as attractive as anything you have ever experienced, right?

There are several people like this in my life, and when things seem to be going haywire, I just want to be around them. It is not because they can necessarily change my reality, but they always help me refresh my perspective. Such people radiate the peace of God. Their tangible execution of standing on His Word allows those around them to witness the transforming power of peace. It is their time spent with Jesus that has developed a sound spirit that is no longer affected by the uncertainties they see. Eyes focused on Jesus, heart anchored deep in the promises of His Word, they become a steady presence in a trendy world.

Do you consider yourself to be a person of peace? Do you find yourself easily overwhelmed? Have you ever considered that what you are currently pursuing is really a deeper sense of peace? Training ourselves in godliness is opening up our desires and letting God have His way in us, over us, and through us. Our prideful spirits tend to have fantastic ideas of how to achieve such peace, usually through the avenues of comfort and control. But what we soon realize is those people we crave being around who walk in such peace had decided to surrender. Through submission to God, laying it all at His feet, we finally taste the fulfillment we exhausted ourselves trying to find.

There is nothing richer than a life of peace. It quickly prioritizes our time, directs our gaze, and establishes a foundation that can withstand even the fiercest of storms. To be people of peace—what if that became our goal?

Prayer

Hey Jesus, thank You for the perfect and complete peace You offer me. It surpasses all understanding. Help me to reflect this peace to others and myself, continually realigning my thoughts and recentering myself in You. In Jesus' name,

AMEN.

A Life of Worship

**Ascribe to the LORD the glory due His name;
worship the LORD in the splendor of His holiness.**

PSALM 29:2 NIV

We usually think of music when the word worship is mentioned. Hands raised, voices singing,
giving praise to Jesus. And while this picture is
not incorrect, it is merely one form of our worship. However, our worship is far more about the
object of our praise, the King of kings, than it is
about the avenue or portal in which we express it.

Worshiping God is possible through music, prayer, adventure,
skill, sacrifice, and many other things that consume our time. It is
the sign of a responsive heart to a loving Father. When we realize the
depravity of our sin, understand the depths of His grace, and experience
His daily decision to pursue us and use us, it is impossible not to worship.
It is in this revelation that our entire lives become worship; we remain in
constant awe of the fact that the King of kings chose us, uses us, and loves
us despite ourselves.

The hard thing about worship is that we often get so caught up in how
it looks or in how we look that our attention transitions to a self-focused
performance or ritual. But our God is not impressed with how a prayer
sounds, how well we sing, or what we create if we are not allowing Him to
intimately speak to our hearts in the process. But when we allow Him to get
close, Spirit to spirit, and fully immerse ourselves in the power and beauty
of our Savior, our spirit can't help but shine.

Our Sunday experiences are a part of worship, but they are certainly not all of it. Worship involves our thoughts, words, and actions on a daily basis—both at home and in our workplace. The way we live every part of our lives reveals whether we have come to understand this lifestyle of worship. Jesus did not ask for a slot on our schedule; He invites us to surrender it all and taste the richness of living hope in our everyday, mundane, trivial, and seemingly unimportant tasks. He desires us to perpetually open ourselves to His loving hands because we trust His heart.

Many times, our pursuit of a more Spirit-filled life is focused far too much on what we are doing to please Him. Rather, if we would wholly give ourselves to rightly seeing Him, our actions would have no choice but to follow. While spiritual disciplines are certainly a necessity, Jesus wants our worship because He wants us to fall in love with Him. And when we fall in love with Him, life will turn to color as He makes His presence known everywhere we go.

Prayer

Hey Jesus, thank You for everything that You are, everything that You do, and everything that You give. Help me rid myself of me so that I can fully worship You. Great is Your faithfulness. In Jesus' name,

AMEN.

The Waiting Room

As for me, I will look to the LORD; I will wait for
the God of my salvation; my God will hear me.

MICAH 7:7 ESV

We all know the feeling of having to wait on
something. The more we want it, the slower the
clock ticks and we feel desperate to get our hands
on that thing, have that prayer be answered, or
arrive at our destination on time. The waiting room
feels like a delay we don't have time for as we plead
with God, "Lord, don't You see I have been patient?
Where are You?"

We seek God during the waiting, thinking that our answer is on
the other side of our waiting; however, it is often the detour itself that
becomes the blessing. In the waiting we ask, "Why is this happening or not
happening?"; "What is God asking of me?"; and "Is there anything holding me back from moving forward?" In our searching for answers we lean
into His instruction and sit at His feet. Our time spent talking with Jesus
to find the solution reminds us that He is our solution, He knows the time
frame, and He is fully aware of our hopes and dreams.

We should not wait to withhold our praise until we get to the other side
because we learn the process is the point. Life will consist of many moments
in which patience will have to be exerted, and it is through the discipline of
celebration and the act of praise that we will find release instead of holding
our breath. We must decide to lift our hands, raise our voices, and show
up in the waiting room, believing that whatever is on the other side of our
waiting is good.

The waiting room does not mean the death of our dreams; rather, it is often the incubator. As we search His heart, He refines ours. The game of waiting leads us to the end of ourselves as we become forced to answer the question "Is He trustworthy?" To keep the faith during these times of waiting, we must take the time to remember His character. When we look to the altars of our past and survey His fingerprints in our current circumstances and in the stories of the Bible, we see that failure, abandonment, and dishonesty have never been part of His track record.

To truly experience peace on this side of the promise, we must ask the question, "Even if this does not happen as I envision it, will I keep believing He knows best?" When we can earnestly say yes, we experience the freedom of the present, knowing that whatever comes from His hands is always for our best. Fear-defying joy is found in doing the holy, hard work that is only possible in the waiting room.

Prayer

Hey Jesus, thank You for Your perfect timing and alignment with all things. Help me to surrender any doubt and fully put my trust in You. Remind me that it is in the waiting that You refine me. My eyes are open. In Jesus' name,

AMEN.

Flexible Faith

Yet You, LORD, are our Father. We
are the clay, You are the potter; we
are all the work of Your hand.

ISAIAH 64:8 NIV

Could any of us have ever predicted the
COVID-19 pandemic? Obviously, it caught
all of us off guard and provided no mercy as
it impacted our personal and professional lives.
Although we would never have preferred the method
in which we had to adapt, the silver lining to the uncertainty was that we all quickly realized that we are not in
control. It forced us to reevaluate, recalibrate, and recenter
ourselves in truth and seek what was next. Plans were forced to
change, and disappointment was definitely rampant; however, in God's
grace, He opened our eyes to the power of surrendering to Him and adapt-
ing in whatever way is necessary.

Flexible faith is willing to move its feet because it knows that what God has
ahead of it is better than anything that's behind it. Flexible faith is willing
to let go of anything that is entangling it so that its hands are open to what
God is doing. Flexible faith is willing to be available to God in whatever
capacity He asks because it knows that is ultimately where fulfillment is
found—not through comfort but by obedience.

When we are malleable, we are able to bend toward whatever God is asking of us and revealing to us along the way. We do not marry ourselves to
our own plans because we trust that God's plans are always better. However, being flexible doesn't mean we commit to everything presented to
us or that we are forced always to bend; it means that we have a strong

enough foundation to be able to respond to the nudges from God without questioning our ability to sustain. It is when we refuse to bend to God's will that we eventually break.

What does this kind of flexibility look like in our everyday lives? Sometimes it means that we give grace to our spouse or family member when plans don't perfectly align with our schedule or someone is running late. Sometimes it means being willing to do the non-preferential things in our jobs because resources are low and labor is short. Other times it means something much larger, like moving to a different city or stepping out of our comfort zones when God asks us to do so. However it looks, this ability to be adaptable always points to the place of our confidence—Jesus. In a culture of self-serving and self-preserving, choosing the narrow way means a willingness to sacrifice our own desires so that others may know Jesus.

What must we not be flexible about? Standing on the Word of God and believing in His character no matter how gloomy things feel around us. When we are firm about these things, they will provide the core structure we need to be strong, able, and dependable in the midst of change, unwavering in our mission but flexible in how we get there.

Prayer

Hey Jesus, thank You for the situations and moments that force me to bend because they remind me that when I am found in You, I will not break. Help me be flexible instead of fearful. Your grace is sufficient. In Jesus' name,

AMEN.

When we are malleable, we are able to bend toward whatever God is asking of us and revealing to us along the way. We do not marry ourselves to our own plans because we trust that God's plans are always better.

CLEERE CHERRY REAVES

Keep a Loose Grip

My son, give Me your heart, and
let your eyes observe My ways.
PROVERBS 23:26 NKJV

Reflect back on when you learned hand-writing, especially cursive. Do you remember how you learned? Hands glued to the pencil, trying with all your might to do it perfectly, but sure to slip up. Then, your teacher or your mom would come alongside you, wrap his or her hands around your hand, and guide your hand forward. Although your fingers were the ones touching the pencil, it was more or less your helper who was doing the writing, right?

It is the same way as we learn to be like Jesus. Through our striving, we often try to achieve the desired results by trial and error, luck, or extravagant practice. However, it is only through our submission that we see the words begin to flow. As our hands relax and our muscles become less tense, we start to catch on to how to form the characters. We begin to think we are the ones doing the writing or the guiding, but it is always through the hand of the One holding us that our lettering, or rather our lives, models what we long for—goodness, love, joy, fulfillment, and so on.

The way we radiate Jesus is through His radiance already happening to us and in us. He is not waiting for us to become the perfect student; when we choose to believe in Him, He wraps His hand around ours and whispers, "Just follow My lead." Though we think we know the sentences we want to write and the way we want them to look, only He knows the pathway to fulfillment and the richness of what is not yet down on paper. It is our desire to tightly grip and white-knuckle the pencil that often keeps us from experiencing progress as we let our pride, fear, or insecurity keep us from giving Him complete control. Contrary to what we previously thought, it is not in leading that we find freedom but in following the One who knows the way.

Just like handwriting, the mere action of saying we want to learn handwriting will not be sufficient. We must grab the pen and be willing to surrender perfection in order to make progress. With Jesus, our desire to love God remains only a statement until we surrender to His will for our lives. Bringing our mess, posturing ourselves before Him, and making ourselves available to Him, we watch as He guides us in the way of the everlasting.

Prayer

Hey Jesus, thank You for the way You pursue me and mold me, despite my pride and my stubbornness. Help me to surrender everything to You, fully trusting Your heart to lead me in the way of abundance. Hands loosened, help me choose freedom. In Jesus' name,

AMEN.

Even When We Cannot See

**The night is far gone; the day is at hand.
So then let us cast off the works of
darkness and put on the armor of light.**

ROMANS 13:12 ESV

It's easy to be kind when those around us are
extending warmth. It feels good and expected to
be people of faith when things are looking up, our
prayers seem to be heard, and life seems like it is on
our side. But what about when our backs are against
the wall, our prayers seem to be falling on deaf ears,
and every time we try to stand back up, the waves crash
again? What then?

But here's what we must remember: There is so little that we know and
so much that we do not see. When the world around us feels chaotic or
when it seems that darkness is winning, that is precisely the time when we
must be the light.

Matthew 5:16 calls us to shine so that others may see and know our Father
in heaven. The Author of hope resides in us, which means that we can
carry hope with us, no matter what our circumstances may be or how
gloomy the world feels. This is the time when others are looking to us,
and we have a great opportunity. If we continue to pursue peace and love
remains our banner, they will know we are trusting in the One we cannot
see, and because of that, our lives are filled with light.

Faith does not offer a guarantee of comprehension or a lack of hardship;
rather, it secures our safety in the midst of any uncertainty or danger we
may face. The opposition is certain—it will occur. However, the divine

hand of God, the intimacy of Jesus, and the guidance of the Holy Spirit are also certain. In fact, it is the dullness of the world that highlights the clarity of Christ. It is in the pit that the hope of glory inspires perseverance.

Will we radiate trust even when the world feels dim? Will we believe God is at work when things feel stagnant? Will we speak promise over hopelessness even when it's hard? If we will, we will get a front-row seat to watching light prevail over darkness every single time.

Prayer

Hey Jesus, thank You for being the light of my life and the hope of glory. When life feels hard, pull me close and help me focus on You. Though darkness looms, Your light is always greater. With You, we always prevail. In Jesus' name,

AMEN.

A Seat at the Table

He brought me to the banqueting house,
and his banner over me was love.

SONG OF SOLOMON 2:4 ESV

Imagine a table. A long, sturdy, well-built table with ornate details and chairs fit for a king. It is covered in the finest linens and set with dishes of every size. And the food? How does one even describe it! It is perfectly delicious. It does not leave you lethargic but fills you up to go forth. The richest of flavors and an abundant supply, it seems like a dream.

This is the feast our heavenly Father has prepared for us. He invites us to eat with Him on a daily basis, to drink from His well and taste of His goodness. Unlike all other places we sit or pleasures we delight ourselves in, this is the only one that does not leave us longing. He sacrificed everything so that we could sit, but there is only one catch: He will not force us to eat. He can, but He won't. He allows us to choose. We can talk about this feast all day long, but if we do not take the time to sit down and eat, what do we truly know of its goodness other than the perception we have created?

This ability to decide what we will devote ourselves to is God's unfathomable grace in action. He could force us to eat, knowing it would lead us back to the table. But He wants us to desire it; He longs for us to find our value and sustenance at His table. And though He knows we will eat and forget His goodness sometimes, He never gives our seat away.

So, will we participate in the feast or just marvel at it? To radiate the love and mercy of Christ, we must eat and drink with Him and know Him to be true. It is a feast meant to be devoured not only on holidays but as a daily occurrence. There is no need to store up food or fear for tomorrow; the table will be present and our seat will be waiting.

When we taste food that actually fills us up, we will know what it means to be satisfied; this new holy expectation will help us recognize when we reach for things that are hollow and meaningless. As we come to the table and sit with the Father, partaking in the way of abundance, we will experience deeper conviction to live a life intentionally fortifying our soul with good things.

Prayer

Hey Jesus, thank You for inviting us to Your table, no matter how long we've been away. Help us to stop chasing meaningless things and to fill our soul with lasting nutrients. We want to participate with You in inviting others to the table where richness is found. In Jesus' name,

AMEN.

Preparing for Promise

*Therefore, preparing your minds for action,
and being sober minded, set your hope
fully on the grace that will be brought to
you at the revelation of Jesus Christ.*

I PETER 1:13 ESV

We have all seen the glow that a newly engaged
couple or an expectant mama exhibits, right? It
has nothing to do with their new skincare regimen
or a recently acquired routine that gives them this
glow; rather, it is as though you can look at them and
tell they are preparing for something beautiful and significant. The future husband and wife are anticipating their
vows and the excited mother will soon hold her baby, and as they
both prepare to receive these promises, they become radiant. Will the
promise bring transition? Sure. Will their prayers for preparation often
include the human emotions of anxiety and impatience? Yes! But as they
position themselves to receive the promise of what is next, Jesus infuses
them with a special hope and gives them guidance until it comes to pass.

Isn't it the same for us? We are all eagerly awaiting the return of our King.
But all along the way—during the time of preparation and process—we
have the ability to radiate the joy of walking toward that promise! Keeping
our minds fastened on His return provides us with the sustenance to keep
going in the here and now. This anticipation should comfort us but also
awaken our minds to action. The time to prepare for His arrival is now, not
in a gimmicky way but in a way that realizes the importance of the season
that is to come! With a new baby, there is no possible way to conceive how
joyous and in awe our hearts will feel, and the truth and anticipation of

Jesus' return should bring us even greater joy! For the One who made the world and gives us the very emotion of joy is returning for us. This revelation should bring us the greatest amount of peace and also sober us into prioritizing what truly matters.

The beautiful but hard thing about preparation is that it rids us of anything we don't need for the journey ahead. God's promises are the hope of our lives, but they also bring about the refining of our souls. As we pray and as we position and posture ourselves so that we can carry the promise once received, the love of Jesus radiates through us. Like a mother excitedly awaiting the birth of her baby, we realize the importance of the current season, knowing that what awaits us is greater than we could ever imagine. Because we know, as with any promise, it is only by grace that the preparation phase was ever a possibility in the first place.

Prayer

Hey Jesus, thank You for the hope of glory and the promise of eternity that You have given us. Help me cultivate this spirit of anticipation and let it permeate my being. Prepare my heart in holiness. In Jesus' name,

AMEN.

The Way We Run

Let me run loose and free, celebrating God's
great work, every bone in my body laughing,
singing, "God, there's no one like You."
PSALM 35:9 THE MESSAGE

Have you ever watched a race and thought, *Look! That guy knows he is going to win*? Even if his feet feel weary and his strength begins to dwindle, he carries a zest in his soul that can be seen from the stands. It is as if he started the race knowing the end result. The truth is, this is how we should run this race of life. Our victory has been sealed in the heavens, and our rewards have never been up for question. These truths are amazing, but they're life-changing only if we apply them.

Since we are naturally competitive and comparative people, it's hard to understand that our pace was intended to be gauged not by the one beside us but rather by the One in front of us. Our story will always look different from the stories of those around us. Each story pulls together a person's background, gifts, struggles, family life, temperament, and character to formulate a path that is impossible to replicate. When we fix our eyes on Jesus, we receive the energy we need around the curves of the track, the self-control we need to keep our body and eyes forward, and the hope we need to put one foot in front of the other. The strategy to keep going is to remember constantly that our victory has been sealed.

If we are Jesus-followers, then the point of our race is to look like Him and tell others about Him. The more that our pace is synonymous with the rhythm of grace and the more our mission is aligned with that of heaven, the more others will understand true victory. The beautiful thing about fighting the good fight of faith is that we know the end result, just like the runner in his race. That is us! Our road map may be uncertain, but our destination is heaven. This truth allows us to persist, even when the battle feels hopeless. We are not operating from the mindset of "I hope I can get up"; we are acting out of the reality of life with Jesus that says, "His strength will sustain me; I know how this ends."

Let's ask ourselves this: If we know we have the victory and we understand that we are not running alone, is there anything that should make us throw in the towel? Sure, we will have moments when that is tempting. Of course we will get out of breath, be discouraged by our slowness, and question our ability to endure, but may we remind our feet that Jesus said, "It is finished." When the end feels out of sight and our weakness sets in, let's lean in. The Giver of our health and Restorer of our energy has His eyes on us, and He is coaching us until we cross the finish line and embrace Him. May we run like we know this is true!

Prayer

Hey Jesus, thank You for showing up for me and sustaining me in this race of life. Help me persist and keep going even when I am weary from the race. Keep my gaze on You and increase my awareness of Your presence. I am strong in You. In Jesus' name,

AMEN.

Nature's Reset

Worthy are you, our LORD and God,
to receive glory and honor and power,
for you created all things, and by your
will they existed and were created.

REVELATION 4:11 ESV

We see it all around us. The sunrise wakes us up
as the birds chirp and greet us before our days
begin. The consistency of its presence reminds us
that no matter the uncertainties that life throws our
way, fresh mercy will always await us and the sun shall
rise again. The lush hydrangeas bloom and cover our
yards as the wild oaks and magnolia trees cast their shade.
The seasonality of the flowers and the color of the leaves are a
visual reminder of the seasons that we will walk through—some may
feel harder than others, but all are necessary for our growth. Our roots are
always revealed when the change comes and we are reminded of what
sustains us—the hope of glory.

The ocean waves crash along the shoreline, and the vastness of the sea
extends for miles. The tide patterns, the life the ocean supports, and the
way the blues change colors, revealing the different depths—it is magnificent. Much like the transitions in our own lives, the waves continue to come
no matter who stands in their way. Like pearls in oyster shells that toss and
turn until their true beauty can be revealed, we are refined through enduring the hardship, not by escaping it.

The mountain's peak surpasses the fog in the sky, and its snow-covered tip
is picturesque. The mountaintop view is indescribable, but there is no sub-
stitute for the hard work it takes to get there. Our lives are a journey, and we

must learn to find joy along the way. Step by step, we begin to discover that the perseverance, grit, and strength gained with each step were actually the point of it all. The view at the top is a bonus.

Nature shows the splendor of the Lord on full display. It is full of all kinds of different forms, timelines, and habitats. It showcases the brilliance of God by its mere existence. His handiwork requires no preparation to exhibit beauty—it must just simply be. Everything we see radiates the power, wisdom, and love of Jesus.

When we forget who is in control or we find ourselves too much in our own heads, getting out in nature always provides a quick restart. We are reminded that He is in control, His creativity is unmatched, and His hands are always at work. Noticing how the Creator so obviously radiates in the world around us often helps recenter us as we remember that His fingerprints are everywhere.

Prayer

Hey Jesus, thank You for the beauty that is so apparent around me. Your fingerprints are seen in every space, and Your brilliance is vast in expression. Remind me to get outside, open my eyes, and be sensitive to the blessings that You've made. In Jesus' name,

AMEN.

Reevaluating Our Rays

For this purpose I have raised you up, to show you my power, so that my name may be proclaimed in all the earth.

EXODUS 9:16 ESV

When we think of the word *radiate*, we often think about the sun and what it does. Think about an image or icon of a sun; it sends out rays, right? Whether consciously or subconsciously, we are always sending out something—whether that be rays of kindness, ripples of impatience, or riptides of frustration. The way that we carry ourselves, the nature of our responses to others, and the way we speak, think, and act are all emitting something.

Sometimes we presume that just because we have been labeled or aligned with a specific entity—such as "I am a Christian"—we inherently send out what that signifies. In other words, we think the fruit of the Spirit is automatic. If we are children of God, then goodness is our go-to response, right? However, what we send out is a direct result of what we let in. If we are filling our minds with worry and crowding our hearts with the pressures from Instagram, it will be difficult to radiate the joy and peace of God. If we are surrounding ourselves with people who don't prioritize His instruction, it will be much harder to walk in obedience.

Spiritual disciplines, such as prayer, reading the Word, and worship are the practical ways that we can recalibrate and realign ourselves with truth. If we want to send out love, then we must first know love—the person of love, Jesus. If we desire to deploy courage, then understanding how warriors of faith like David, Paul, and Moses were courageous can serve as altars for us to stand upon for our own lives. If we want to radiate joy, then rejoicing with praise music on our lips is a helpful practice. These spiritual disciplines ensure our freedom and ability to send out the hope of Jesus.

When we second-guess what we are sending out, we can ask those we are frequently around, What do you feel when you are around me? Do I help you remember truth? Do I send out grace and forgiveness easily? It is not that we ask these questions in search of affirmation; however, getting honest about who we are and what we radiate allows us to see things through a more accurate lens. This is not to layer on the shame, bring offense, or discourage us; rather, it positions us to prayerfully consider how we are reflecting our Savior.

The sun is known to be a giver of light and a helper toward joy. It heats the cold days and reflects off the ocean. It makes no qualms about what it is or what it isn't. What do our lives say, and what rays are we sending out?

Prayer

Hey Jesus, thank You for the way You allow me to step back and evaluate what I am sending out. Help me radiate Your love and develop a countenance of joy. I want to send out Your light and let my life sing of Your splendor. In Jesus' name,

AMEN.

Nothing before Him

Seek the Kingdom of God above all
else, and live righteously, and He will
give you everything you need.

MATTHEW 6:33 NLT

When we hear the word "idol," we often imagine some tiki-like statute, right? Or when we
think of it in a spiritual sense, we assume it has
to be something really big and invasive or tangible.
However, an idol simply means anything that is caus-
ing distance between us and Jesus. This can manifest
itself as an addiction or stronghold, a struggle with worry,
a constant preoccupation with money, or even something
good like serving others. The act itself is not what deems it an
idol, it is the attention we give it that robs us of our time with Jesus that
makes it so.

Jesus mourns our separation from Him. Do we truly understand that?
While He hates that these idols often stem from pride, fear, or insecurity,
He is most saddened by the fact that they are caused by us reaching for life
outside of Him. His willingness to abolish anything that steals our focus
affirms His crazy love for us. Because He knows that the peace, adventure,
joy, and abundance we are searching for can only be discovered when pursuing Him, He will often allow us to get to the end of ourselves and our
frivolous pursuits so that we see He really is the only source of good things.

To see the jealousy of God any other way than through the avenue of love
is to assume that there is anything better than Him. Let me explain: If
we assume His jealousy is because He fears competition, then we are acting as though there is anything that can compete. If we presume that He

craves our attention to solidify His throne, then we do not have a rightful view of God. He does not need us, we need Him. Therefore, His preservation of our souls can only be for our protection and out of His love; His jealousy for our attention is truly another form of grace, as it vigorously fights for us to realize that apart from Him, our feelings of emptiness will persist.

All of this should not scare us or shame us, but rather lead us right back to Him. The greatest wisdom we show is through the act of repentance, the revelation of what is true, the discipline of turning around, and the grace of walking up to the front door of our Father's house. We no longer have to wait in rebellion, barefoot and cold, wondering if we belong inside; we were created for this moment. This is our house because we are His children; He was just yearning for us to walk in our God-given identity.

Prayer

Hey Jesus, thank You for the way You fight for my soul and protect my heart. Apart from You, there is no good thing. Keep my gaze on You and help me rid myself of anything that separates me from You. In Jesus' name,

AMEN.

I Can't Hear You

My child, listen to what I say, and treasure
my commands. Tune your ears to wisdom,
and concentrate on understanding.

PROVERBS 2:1–2 NLT

Growing up, I remember when my mom would be asking me a question or providing direction for the day ahead and I would ask, "What did you say, Mom? I couldn't hear you." I would keep the volume up on the television in front of me and ask her to repeat it, knowing that I would still be struggling to figure out what exactly she was saying. We would both end up frustrated, but for different reasons. My mom would be aggravated with the lack of awareness to turn the television down and her need to repeat herself. I would be stubbornly annoyed that I couldn't hear both at once, knowing that her words were important but they were going to force me to turn down what I had tuned into already.

This is such an elementary example, but I think simplicity is necessary when discussing this point: If we want to hear the voice of God, we are going to have to turn down the volume on what we are listening to currently. Though we would love to hear both at the same time, we are not honoring God when we ask Him to show up but we aren't willing to give up what's comfortable and entertaining us at the moment.

How does this tendency usually show up in our everyday lives? We are notorious for trying to multitask, including when it comes to spending time with Jesus. We want to receive His direction without having to discipline ourselves to hear His voice. However, He is not going to get louder to compete with the voices and distractions we have turned up in our lives; He is going to ask us to get quiet so that we can hear the One who matters. This tendency to want to hear everything at once is glorified in our noisy culture, but if we desire the posture of peace as we say we do, we will have to make it a practice to only listen to one channel at a time.

Whether our attention is preoccupied with something else because of the fear of missing out or whether we have created a habit of living reactively rather than responsively, we must decide who gets the loudest say in our lives. Because the goal is not to always have to turn down what we are listening to, the hope is to seek Him first. The only way to a fruitful life is to stay dialed into Jesus and keep His truth as the main stream of input we have flowing into our hearts. When we do this, we will hear His direction, receive His affirmation, and trust His voice wherever He leads.

Prayer

Hey Jesus, thank You for Your patience with my spirit. Help me to turn down the noise and distractions in my life so that Your voice becomes clear. Keep me in tune with Your truth. Your instruction is life, and You deserve all my attention. In Jesus' name,

AMEN.

Stop the Scrolling

It is the Spirit who gives life; the flesh is no help at all. The words that I have spoken to you are spirit and life.

JOHN 6:63 ESV

This is not a devotion about scrolling.
I repeat, this is not a devotion about scrolling.
Wait, yes it is.

Whether on our phones, computers, iPads, or whatever it may be, we are a world consumed by what is on the screen. We are more inclined to realize we have lost our phones than we are to realize we have lost our peace. With our hands always holding a phone or it being easily in reach, our boredom or longing is replaced by scrolling whatever site or feed temporarily entertains us, unaware of what we are even looking for as we scroll.

The problem is, we are searching for love in a world full of likes and wondering why we feel lost. We know it's not the way because we were made by the Way Himself, and yet, we keep returning to it. We have become really good at deceiving ourselves, convincing our own minds that we aren't comparing our lives to others. Yet, three days later, we have an emotional breakdown because we feel behind in our lives and discouraged by our surroundings. But what was it that told us we are behind? And where did that anxiety stem from? We thought we were just satisfying our curiosity but soon realize we were feeding our envy, our discomfort, and our insecurity. We realize we have been searching for meaning, purpose, and fulfillment.

How do we stop the scrolling and dig into something that lasts? We literally stop scrolling. We set our phones down and we open the Bible. We place our charger away from our bed so our hands grab for His Word first thing in the morning rather than the timeline updates from the world. We have date night and leave our phones in the car. We set time limits on the social applications on our phone. We put it on airplane mode when we are with family or friends if possible.

We do whatever is necessary to realign our thoughts, recalibrate our minds, and restore our souls to Him. If we do not make some abrupt changes in the habits and practices we actually have, we run the chance of becoming believers with good intentions and little faith. We have the library of life change available at our fingertips in the Word of God. It is the ticket to the greatest adventure park, the answer to all of life's questions, the key to security, and the keeper of peace. How drastically would our lives change if we reached for it as often as we reach for our phones? That's not radical; that's intentional. And possible.

Prayer

Hey Jesus, thank You for the reminder that the "normal" around me is not what You desire for my life. Help me stop reaching for my phone and go to the throne instead. Hidden in You is where life is found. In Jesus' name,

AMEN.

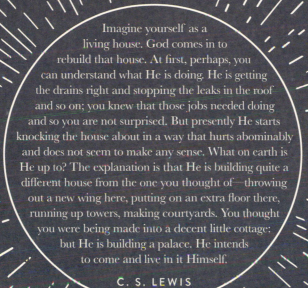

Imagine yourself as a
living house. God comes in to
rebuild that house. At first, perhaps, you
can understand what He is doing. He is getting
the drains right and stopping the leaks in the roof
and so on; you knew that those jobs needed doing
and so you are not surprised. But presently He starts
knocking the house about in a way that hurts abominably
and does not seem to make any sense. What on earth is
He up to? The explanation is that He is building quite a
different house from the one you thought of—throwing
out a new wing here, putting on an extra floor there,
running up towers, making courtyards. You thought
you were being made into a decent little cottage:
but He is building a palace. He intends
to come and live in it Himself.

C. S. LEWIS

Lay It All Out There

Then you will call on Me and come and pray to Me, and I will listen to you.

JEREMIAH 29:12 NIV

How do we learn to pray? Many of us feel like we don't know how or question if what we are currently doing is the "right way."

Surely it is silly to talk to such a mighty and powerful God about the trivial details of our lives. However, this is precisely what He wants to hear. To believe that certain contents of our hearts are not substantial enough to include in our prayers reveals that we not only don't understand prayer but also have misinterpreted the One we pray to.

C. S. Lewis tells us to "lay before Him what is in us, not what ought to be in us."* If our prayers, the most intimate time we have with the Father, feel like striving, then what avenue will be a safe haven for our authentic selves? Prayer allows us to bring every morsel before Him—the places of our unbelief, the sources of our anxiety, the friendship we are worried about, or the snooty remark from our neighbor we can't seem to let go. When we speak frankly with our Father, we allow our souls to feel known and seen, even if He was already aware of it all.

The only reason we would withhold the honest thoughts of our hearts is if we thought they didn't matter to Him or that He is not capable of changing them. However, if we don't believe He will intervene in the mundane and the ordinary, why would we invite Him into the big and the extraordinary?

How does a child learn to have a conversation? They talk. How do we learn to have a conversation with God? We talk to Him. And we listen.

Prayer is like an incubator for spiritual growth, and the effect of spiritual growth is displaying the radiance of God. We learn more about the heart of the One who made us, and in our communication with Him, we point to heaven.

Let us not be discouraged by the very vehicle that takes us straight to His feet. If we struggle to desire to pray, that in itself is a prayer! Do you see? All is welcome. Nothing is trivial. Transformation is absolute. We do not need a fancy way to pray, a higher degree to discern, or a "better" past to be eligible to be heard by Jesus. The proper way to pray to God is merely that: to pray.

May we find ourselves so hidden in Him that we hide nothing from Him. That is a life of peace.

Prayer

Hey Jesus, thank You for bending down to hear my prayers and desiring to hear my voice. Nothing is too big or too small, Lord. Help me not to concentrate on the logistics of prayer but rather just fix my eyes on You so that I can learn Your heart. In Jesus' name,

C. S. Lewis, *Letters to Malcolm: Chiefly on Prayer* (Eugene; Harvest Books, 1973), p. 22.

AMEN.

Talking to Myself

When we think about the conversations that we
have, we quickly think of those we have with others. However, experts agree that no one is more
influential in our daily lives than we are. Regardless
of whether sound is coming out of our mouths, we
are in constant conversation with ourselves. Whether
it be while we are grocery shopping, driving down the
highway, or getting a quick workout in, we are formulating
thoughts at all moments about all kinds of things. Even when we
are in the company of others or involved in intense conversation with
those around us, we still have a thought wheel circling in our own brains.

What if we had a transcript of all the conversations we have with ourselves? If our thoughts were typed out for all to see, what conclusions
would be drawn? What do we tend to focus on, think about, and struggle
with? When does our mind tend to race without caution and get anxious
inside? What keeps us up at night or motivates us to stay on the treadmill?
Are we usually dealing with an inner critic or a kindness coach?

We all have big dreams, great desires to make something of our lives, and
hopes for where we will be in twenty years. However, the only way that we
will be able to serve wholeheartedly and find deep purpose in the here and
now is if we deal with some things on the inside. Sure, it's hard. Compli-
cated. Even we ourselves don't realize how quickly we make assumptions,
practice self-condemnation, or let the snowball roll until we are forced to

step back and evaluate. Since we talk to ourselves the most, we are the people most responsible for the choices we make. We are the ones who decide what is truth and what is trash; we are the ones who choose to react in anger or respond with tenderness. And most importantly, if we don't like the place we are, maybe we should ask ourselves what we have been repeating over our lives.

What would happen if we prepared for these conversations ourselves? What do I mean by this? Well, we know sunshine and rainbows won't always fill our skies, so how will we talk to ourselves when it rains? What will we tell ourselves to do when we want to walk away from a relationship or a marriage? What dialogue will we revert to when we step on a scale and we don't like the number we see? The Lord has given us His Word to dig into, recite, and rehearse over ourselves.

When the chatter on the inside reflects the truth of Jesus, we begin to radiate the grace of Jesus. As we lavish grace on ourselves, we give it away more freely. Since we will continue to have the most conversations with ourselves, let's make them honest, life-giving, and kind.

Prayer

Hey Jesus, thank You for the ability that You have given me to practice self-discipline in my thought life. Help me to realign my mind with truth and speak to myself with grace and love. Help me see me how You see me. In Jesus' name,

AMEN.

The Invitation of Brokenness

I live in a high and holy place, but also with
the one who is contrite and lowly in spirit.

ISAIAH 57:15 NIV

We come up against the wall often, don't we?
This stark, tall wall between who we want to be
and who we currently feel that we are. And the
more we realize how thick this wall is, the more
frustrating and condemning it feels as we stare at it.
We want to look like Him, but circumstances happen
or life throws fastballs that come right down the pike
and we aren't ready.

It's the moments where we are walking, cup in hand, and someone
or something hits us just right and we spill over. And we don't like what
comes out because we weren't prepared for it. But that overflow? That
humanity? That becomes our invitation.

There's no condemnation or shame as we enter His presence and simply
ask, "Hey, Dad, can You give me Your gentleness? I can't find mine." That
thick, tall, intimidating wall gets destroyed in a moment. The gap between
who we wish we could be and who we currently are is filled. And He meets
us. "I would love nothing more," He says.

Whatever we need for our day, we can ask Him for it. And it won't be our
version, it will be HIS. We have access to the fruit of the Spirit, and they
are rich in flavor, lacking no good thing.

Love. Joy. Peace. Patience. Kindness. Goodness. Faithfulness. Gentleness.
Self-control.

When we want to be cold to others, we can ask for kindness.
When we feel criticism or judgment rising up, we can ask for His compassion.
When we feel our patience wearing thin, we can ask for His gentleness.

In our interactions with others and ourselves, we have the ability to take on His nature. Our humanity becomes our invitation to ask, "Can You give me more of You?"

So, maybe we decide today to stop hating the very thing that brings us to His throne. The thorn in our side, the issue that keeps arising, the part of our personality we can't seem to shake—what if we asked Him to replace that with Him? Pure Jesus. That is what we want to fill the space where we're lacking.

Let's be thankful for the brokenness that brings us to the mirror, asking ourselves, "How did I come to reflect that?" And be thankful that when we come, Jesus looks back at us and says, "I'll help you look just like Me."

Prayer

Hey Jesus, thank You for the brokenness that brings me to Your feet.
Though my humanity can feel difficult and messy, I know it is
the invitation to rid myself of me so that I can reflect You.
In Jesus' name,

AMEN.

Open Your Eyes

Then the eyes of those who see will not be closed, and the ears of those who hear will give attention.

ISAIAH 32:3 ESV

How do our eyes make sense of objects and actually see? The ability to have sight is made possible when a light (such as a lamp) is turned on or when light reflects off the surface of an object and into our eyes. It is only when our eyes are open and enlightened that we are able to witness the beauty that lies in front of us.

If we want to be people who radiate the love of Christ, then our eyes must be open, and not just in the natural sense. Because we are children of the Most High King, we have the ability to tap into supernatural powers, including the ability to see beyond what the world sees. When our eyes are enlightened, we are aware of reality and become more in tune with our heavenly perspective.

Through the lens of faith, we believe in miracles before they occur, and we step into the unknown because our God calls us into the deep. This kind of heavenly perspective allows us to not just talk about what happens, but to also participate with God in the miracles, right here, right now.

What if we prayed not for a different view but for a supernatural filter over our circumstances? Open eyes allow for an available heart and willing feet because His faithfulness becomes so obvious. Instead of working to see God, we have to work not to see Him. We do not follow a God who we pray shows up; we serve the King who never leaves the scene. The more we seek to find Him, the greater our courage will become as our confidence anchors itself in His reliability.

As we survey the wonder around us and as we saturate ourselves in glorifying Him, light will reflect off us and we will become radiant in Him. That is His hope for His people and the greatest way we could live—grounded by grace reflecting the light of His love and helping others see. As we seek shelter in Jesus' love, we become beacons of light and help open the eyes of those around us. In doing so, we remember there is nothing greater than pointing others to heaven, where all glory awaits.

Prayer

Hey Jesus, thank You for the supernatural vision You give to Your children, allowing us to operate beyond just what we see and know. Help me to live based on Your faithfulness so that I may give light and help others see. In Jesus' name,

AMEN.

Let's Be Mayonnaise

Finally, brothers and sisters, rejoice! Strive
for full restoration, encourage one another,
be of one mind, live in peace. And the
God of love and peace will be with you.

II CORINTHIANS 13:11 NIV

When you put oil and vinegar into a jar, they naturally separate. Even when they are combined in the same recipe for a dressing, you can shake them up over and over and they will still separate. However, did you know that they are the two main ingredients in mayonnaise? Obviously we can see that they somehow manage to stay together in mayonnaise, but how? The key is an emulsifier, which is a substance that brings these two ingredients together so they become fused, impossible to separate, forming what is commonly termed an emulsion.

When it comes to other people and the relationships around us, Jesus is our emulsifier. As humans, we will always struggle to put down our pride, surrender our desires, and serve others with joy. It's the nature of our humanity. However, when we let Jesus infuse us with the Holy Spirit, we are given His eyes! This allows us to not only see ourselves through the correct lens but to view others through that lens as well. When we accept the covering of Jesus, an emulsion is able to be formed—the coming together of two previously nonblendable beings now able to discover perfect unity in Him. Marriage is the ultimate example of this scenario, in which the two substances blended together are no longer recognizable apart from one another. The two literally become one.

Because the Holy Spirit lives within us, we are able to unify with other believers in a deeper, more profound way. Jesus makes no mistakes. His crafting of our differences was intentional and profound. Two parts of the body are not meant to look the same or have the same function; however, the body is labeled not as a series of parts but as one collective unit. Our heavenly Father desires that we operate in the same way with our brothers and sisters, letting His grace be the emulsifier that breaks past our barriers and opens our eyes to the power of coming together.

Mayonnaise is a relatively polarizing food—people tend to either love it or hate it. However, when the body of Christ functions as the Father intended, it is impossible to not be unified in pursuit. The body of Christ is powerful and persistent; its members show up for each other and the world around them, even when differing political, social, or cultural opinions are represented. Is there someone in your life who seems like oil and you're vinegar? Does your marriage feel more like a war, where you and your spouse are fighting against each other rather than side by side? We can take heart in this! God knew our human side would want to fight against others, so He reminded us of where the true battle lies—it's not against other humans but against the true enemy. As we join hands and become unified in building God's kingdom, we radiate the brilliance of God's melting pot at work.

Prayer

Hey Jesus, thank You for covering each of Your children in Your righteousness—heavenly and pure. Help us to step outside our comfort zones and work to find unity here. You are our common ground, and in You we are all one family. In Jesus' name,

AMEN.

Mission-Minded

I am not ashamed of the gospel, for it is the power of God for salvation to everyone who believes, to the Jew first and also to the Greek.

ROMANS 1:16 ESV

Have you ever been on a mission trip? Here's how it works: You sign up, fundraise, plan, and prepare yourself to go across the world. You literally get on an airplane and travel to a country where you don't speak the language or understand the customs, and you go with the intent of sharing the gospel. Along with your team, you boldly enter these spaces willing to get uncomfortable and meet the needs of others, all for the sake of Jesus. And you work hard to cross whatever hurdles are present so that you can reach people with God's love.

Mission trips tend to open your eyes to what God has for you, and for what He has for those around you—and the experience is amazing. But do you ever wonder why we are so willing to be unashamed on a different continent but we get hesitant at our neighborhood grocery store? Or are we too rushed to actually take the time to stop, notice people, and speak into their lives?

The crazy part about Jesus' life is that so much of His time was filled with "interruptions." There are many Bible stories that begin with "As Jesus was on the way to _____." And in these stories He was interrupted by someone in need. Though He had a destination in mind, Jesus lived mission-minded every moment. There was not a hierarchy of importance in regards to people, and He was constantly returning to the Father in prayer to surrender His own agenda, fully aware that what God had planned was different from what He could see. And when Jesus did speak with others, He wasted no time engaging in truth. He compassionately listened to their pleas and prayers, but His main concern was opening their eyes to the hope of eternity. He was on earth to point to heaven.

How would it look in our own lives if we entered our mundane Mondays and our everyday spaces with vigor, eagerness, and passion to share the gospel? If we knew that above anything and everything else, sharing the love of Jesus was absolutely first priority, would we speak less or more? Would our demeanor be more peaceful? Would we exchange gossip for life-giving conversation? Would we stop wondering if others agreed and just ask them if they know Jesus?

The greatest way that we can spend our time, and the most important way we can spend other people's time, is to get honest about forever. Whether in the grocery store, gym, school, or workplace, may we be willing to walk in boldness and truth, knowing Jesus will grace us with all that we need.

Prayer

Hey Jesus, thank You for the good news—it is literally what saves my soul and preserves my life. Help me to understand the urgency of sharing truth. Give me eyes to see and a heart to reach out. Make me bold. In Jesus' name,

AMEN.

Reach Out to Radiate

Do not neglect to do good and to share what you have, for such sacrifices are pleasing to God.

HEBREWS 13:16 ESV

The nature of something radiating is that whatever is in the center spreads to what is around it. It is generous in nature because the desired intent of its creation is that it does not keep to itself. It finds its sole purpose in receiving its personal supply so that it can have the energy, strength, and sustenance to meet the needs of another.

When someone reaches out to us—whether to extend a congratulations, offer assistance with a specific task, or merely affirm their presence in a time of need—what do we feel? Gratefulness. We feel seen. We feel important. Although we know others are never to be the determinant of our identity or the place where we find our affirmation, knowing someone would take the time to reach out to us helps us feel valued and important. It is the tangible grace of God, as we know that their reaching out is an extension of God's hand.

Regardless of how we respond, we can't help but be touched by their action. When we choose to radiate the kindness and generosity of Christ, we extend our hands and move our feet because that is what He has done for us. When Jesus suffered on the cross, He knew who He was dying for—friends who had betrayed Him, authorities who had defamed him, and a bunch of sinners who would forget Him. And yet, He chose to reach out His arms and put the weight of the world on His shoulders, fully aware that we would never be able to return the favor. He assumed the consequences of our mistakes and offered us the gift of eternity.

What if we made it our mission to reach out to someone in need every Wednesday or take a friend who is quietly struggling to lunch? Our intentional act of kindness doesn't have to be large or world-altering; however, don't be surprised when they express what it does to change their world. Because that's how faithful our Jesus is—He can take our small acts of intentionality and generosity and multiply them beyond measure.

May we give without expectation and show up without being asked, trusting God to cover our needs and give us the courage to knock on the doors of the hearts around us. When we root ourselves in the healthy soil of God's love, we naturally will want to reach out to others in love. True generosity finds its greatest delight in giving without ever expecting anything in return.

Prayer

Hey Jesus, thank You for the cross. You took on Calvary so that I could be free. Help me use that freedom to serve and show up well for others. I want to give without expectation but in anticipation of Your love in action. In Jesus' name,

AMEN.

He's Proud of You

Even before He made the world, God loved us and chose us in Christ to be holy and without fault in His eyes.

EPHESIANS 1:4 NLT

The concept feels foreign to us—that just by nature of who we are, someone is proud of us? That feels too good to be true.

But at the very same time, isn't that just like Jesus? To offer a grace so good and a foundation so firm, that we did nothing to earn, that makes us know it could only come from the hand of our Father?

"And a voice from heaven said, 'This is My Son, whom I love; with Him I am well pleased'" (Matthew 3:17 NIV). This is what God said about Jesus right after He was baptized; Jesus had not yet turned water into wine, healed anyone, or raised anyone from the dead. And yet God chose this particular language—"This is My Son." He was claiming Him, firmly stamping His identity and reminding Jesus of who He is. Then God continued and said, "With Him I am well pleased."

Because Jesus is the Son of God, He walked in automatic security. Total reliance. Complete affirmation from His Father. This same truth goes for us too. Because of Whose we are, we never need to prove we are worthy of His acceptance. No one who belongs to God has to ever prove he or she is fit to be there. When our heritage is Jesus, our inheritance is pure security.

May we be a little kinder to ourselves and others, remembering that it is usually our gentleness, not our criticism, that pulls out greatness. However, regardless of what we say to ourselves or what others say to us, we have already been affirmed by Him. Taking the pressure off our performance allows us to operate in peace and put our best foot forward. Removing the burden of proving our worth gives us the confidence to freely walk forward wherever He calls. He simply delights in us.

Before you landed that job, made the team, felt like a good mom, lost that weight, received public recognition, earned your parents' affirmation, believed in yourself, or ever uttered a word, He was proud of you.

When we let this truth permeate our souls, reaching into the hidden and unseen spaces, we can walk in confidence and trust that He is working in us and through us. Radiating Jesus does not mean erasing all signs of imperfections; rather, it means bringing that brokenness to His feet and believing He will cover all the gaps. When we begin to receive this kind of love and affirmation, we no longer need the world's approval. The love of Jesus supersedes any "likes" we could receive here as we realize that the Creator of the stars made us to shine for Him.

Prayer

Hey Jesus, thank You for the way You see me, believe in me, and speak life over me. Help me stop striving for affirmation and rest in the security of being claimed by You. I do not have to earn Your love; wow, thank You. In Jesus' name,

AMEN.

No Strings Attached

Whoever would be first among you must
be slave of all. For even the Son of Man
came not to be served but to serve, and
to give his life as a ransom for many.

MARK 10:44–45 ESV

Service. How we show up for others, what we
choose to give, and the way that we offer ourselves—what does it look like?

Often we give, and our gift is needed, important, and
valuable.

But we attach strings.
The strings of hopeful reciprocation.
The strings of personal affirmation.
The strings of good moral standing.
The strings of "Jesus, did You see that?"
The strings of our personal mood or emotions toward that person, place,
or circumstance.

All these strings tend to factor into our ability to serve, and in them we lose
the essence of service. Because if we focus more on the reward our service
brings or the reciprocation we hope to receive, the motivation for our service is already compromised.

True service does not discriminate based on the size of the task or the
reception of the effort. Because the point is worship, this service is not married to results. True service is a lifestyle—not a reaction, a sudden whim
to give based on a high, or a guilt-ridden response to someone in need. It

is the response to the revelation of all that we have already been given, including relationships, hope, and eternal life. How is it that He has lavished such grace on us and yet we expect tally marks for our self-righteous attempts to earn His favor? Or we work to guarantee a strong moral perception from those watching?

We can't earn it! We can merely surrender to it—give our lives to it—and show up in the inconvenient, tough, trying moments because He gave everything to us.

No matter how impatient, rushed, or frustrated we feel, we commit our hearts to being present. To stopping, seeing, and serving whomever, whenever, and wherever He asks.

This kind of humility is the fabric of a true servant leader and the surest way others will become curious about our God. Because when we stop focusing on titles and decide to pick up the towel, eager to wash the feet of anyone who needs it, we discover the key to our authority.

We don't serve people because we HAVE to or because we SHOULD; we serve because we CHOOSE to. And then deep joy fills our souls.

Prayer

Hey Jesus, thank You for being the greatest example of a servant. Help us walk with the same humility and love that You did. Remove our need for affirmation, reciprocation, or expectation, and let us truly serve. Such a life unearths the greatest joy. In Jesus' name,

AMEN.

Pain Points

Just as we share abundantly in the suffering of Christ, so also our comfort abounds through Christ.

II CORINTHIANS 1:5 NIV

Radiating pain happens in our bodies when pain starts in one place and is connected to a nerve that then carries this pain along a nerve path. Any part of the body that is connected to this nerve path will be in danger of experiencing that pain. No further injury is necessary; it's just the connection of the two that transfers the pain.

This principle is much the same in our own hearts—what we are connected to affects what we experience. We are often guilty of radiating certain characteristics or sending out negativity because of the sources we are linked to or the places where we connect. As much as we would like to press a button and emit sunshine at all moments, sometimes we must realize what we are radiating in order to diagnose and relieve the pain points on our radar and in our system.

We all have deep roots and thought patterns we have watered for years. These thoughts create habits and patterns that we are often subconsciously aware of, not realizing the negative effect on ourselves and others as we continue in the loop we have been riding. The problem with letting things simmer, stuffing them under the rug, or harboring bitterness is that when we are hurt, we eventually bleed on all those in our path. This pain manifests in unusual ways, dressing itself up as one issue or another, deceiving our own hearts from the true source. For example, we can have a herniated disc in our back, but our greatest pain point can become our legs, as the disc is on the nerve path connected to our sciatic nerve, which runs down our legs. The pain that feels the most urgent is often not the root.

To lessen physical pain, doctors often recommend taking medication to decrease the inflammation. How does inflammation occur? It is the result of our bodies trying to fight off something harmful. This is what happens when we let pain fester in our souls. As it sneakily seeps into the other areas of our lives, our hearts try to fight it off with coping mechanisms, bitterness, increased jealousy, self-rejection, or apathy. These inflame the spirit because our spirit knows the true root and wants us to deal with the actual source of our hurt.

But if we can realign ourselves with truth and reconnect our hearts with His—stepping back on the nerve path His Word instructs—healing can take place. The inner workings of our hearts will have to do some hard work, but it will allow new roots to grow, healthy thought patterns to build, and restoration to take place.

Jesus is the Vine and we are the branches. What we are connected to matters. Let's remain aware of our pain and humbly bring it to Him. He is always the cure.

Prayer

Hey Jesus, thank You for always helping me deal with the root of my pain. You are my healer, my comforter, and my strength. Show me anything I am connected to that is hurting me and help me turn to You. In Jesus' name,

AMEN.

If worship does not propel us into greater obedience, it has not been worship. To stand before the Holy One of eternity is to change.

RICHARD FOSTER

See Ya, Bitterness

You shall not take vengeance or bear a grudge
against the sons of your own people, but you shall
love your neighbor as yourself: I am the LORD.

LEVITICUS 19:18 ESV

He clocked him square in the face. We all ran over, thinking a tooth would be missing or a goose egg had surely formed on his head. Thankfully, all was okay and his cries calmed down as he realized he was okay.

Not even five minutes later, he put his shoes back on and walked back over to the circle of death and started playing again. It was as if the near knockout just minutes prior had not even happened. No bitterness in his actions, a smile on his face, and ready for action!

This has happened countless times with my nephews, and each time I think to myself, "If only I could forgive like that." Granted, the stakes were not crazy high and they are both under the age of six, but it really is such an example of how our heavenly Father wants us to operate in our daily lives. When it comes to forgiveness, we think if we just stop talking about it and move on, it's enough. Or if we decide to put ourselves out there again and risk vulnerability, we have truly forgiven. However, my nephews remind me that until we choose to not only enter back in but do so with joy and expectation, we have not truly forgiven. This doesn't mean we don't move forward in wisdom and discernment, but it does mean that we must show up in life willing to give our all and our best even though we know we will eventually experience pain.

Forgiveness is not only about not rehearsing the past but about participating in the present and preparing ourselves for the future. If we give in to bitterness or we let the experiences of our past keep our hearts hesitant or our feet stagnant, we are still living in what was and not stepping into what can be. The hard part about fully letting go of the past is that justice is not always served on this side of heaven; we do not get to forgive only after we feel the consequences are sufficient. We decide to let go of an offense because it is the way of Jesus. That must be enough for us.

As my nephew dried his eyes, he said, "I want to go play!" His eagerness to return was founded upon his knowing what the present could be if he forgave his brother. Maybe this simple truth is what keeps us from moving forward in forgiveness—we want it to be more complex. But it is simple. As we extend grace to others, we get to drink in the goodness it brings and be an example of Jesus in action.

Prayer

Hey Jesus, thank You for the way You help me forgive others. Help me let any bitterness go so that I can fully embrace the present and be expectant for my future. Grace and justice come from You. In Jesus' name,

AMEN.

Fully Devoted

Let your heart therefore be wholly devoted to the LORD our God, to walk in His statutes and to keep His commandments, as at this day.

I KINGS 8:61 NASB

If your close friends or family were to describe you, what would they say you are devoted to? What are you known for, an "expert" in, or extremely curious about? Think about the ways you spend your time, what you bring up in conversation, and what fills your dreams when you imagine the impossible. We often don't realize what we are devoted to because it has become such a priority and automatic in our lives. Surveying our time, asking those we are close to, and searching the contents of our thoughts help us understand where we place value.

When we say we are "devoted" to a cause, we are usually devoted to it as long as it serves the purposes of our desires or dreams. Our commitment is often linked to results, as we believe the time we give and the resources we extend will produce a particular outcome. However, God does not ask us for this kind of devotion. He longs for us to be so devoted to Him that the outcome is secondary. Our obedience is primary, meaning we are willing to stand firm when things seem shaky, we are willing to give when finances seem uncertain, and we are available to go wherever He sends us no matter what plans we have conceptualized for our lives.

We see this kind of devotion all throughout Scripture, particularly when Mary is told she will give birth to Jesus. Because we know the life, impact, and truth of Jesus, it is easy for us to say, "Well of course she was devoted to that cause—it's Jesus!" However, Mary was a teenage virgin. Before the angel appeared, she received no warning about her life being uprooted. And, her initial response when the angel came and told her that she would give birth to Jesus was total fear. Her brain tried to rationalize and understand, yet in her heart she knew this could only be received through faith.

"'I am the Lord's servant,' Mary answered. 'May your word to me be fulfilled'" (Luke 1:38 NIV). Mary's response surpassed her feelings and her own plans; she recognized her role as a servant and the devotion that this required. She voiced her concerns and surrendered them to the Father, knowing her life would be marked by her obedience, not the outcome of it.

May we live in the way of Mary. Even when our brains wrestle to grasp or our feet are weary to follow, we are servants who are devoted to the King.

Prayer

Hey Jesus, thank You for being a King who is always worthy of our total devotion. Remind us that we are Your servants; help us to seek obedience rather than outcomes. We trust You. In Jesus' name,

AMEN.

Rewrite Your Narrative

**God rewrote the text of my life when I
opened the book of my heart to His eyes.**

PSALM 18:24 THE MESSAGE

We walk into a room and it begins. We survey
how their circle seems closed off and assume
they don't want us to join. We look at what others are wearing and quickly wonder if we are
overdressed or underdressed or what others are
thinking about the way we look. We see someone we
know, quickly reflect on our last interaction, and begin
to think of the conversation we might have. And before we
know it, we have written a narrative about the current situation that is full of assumptions, preconceived notions, and filters.

Do you ever find yourself doing this? What does your narrative usually
sound like? Do you assume you are wanted in the space you're in, that
others are talking about you, or that your appearance sufficiently measures
up to the standards that you have set for yourself and others? What is interesting about our narratives is that no matter the situation, every person is
different. The circumstances can be exactly the same, but due to our child-
hood experience, our current or past struggles, and our overall makeup, we
each craft a different story in our heads.

This narrative can go one of two ways: it either aligns with the truth of
God's Word or it doesn't. The ways in which it aligns can differ, but there
is not much gray area when it comes to this. Oftentimes, we forget to sift it
through the light of truth because we don't even realize we are crafting a
narrative and we assume it is truth. Such presumptions often keep us from
pursuing relationships, feeling valued in a place, experiencing belonging,

or being vulnerable with others. Narratives that don't align with truth keep us from trusting God to protect us, as we seek to self-preserve and self-protect rather than surrender to Him.

What does your current narrative say? Have you asked Jesus what might need to be removed and replaced? If it makes you feel small, insecure, fearful, uncertain, hopeless, or anything that doesn't match the character of God, it's not from Him. Be aware of these thoughts forming and choose to focus on what is true and what is sure.

Narratives are powerful. No matter how yours has led you up to this point, remember that God can rewrite it in a moment's time. Give Him the reins and pen a story that brings glory to the King.

Prayer

Hey Jesus, thank You for bringing attention to my thoughts—good and bad. Help me to let go of assumptions and judgment upon myself or others; I want to craft a narrative that points to Your truth. In Jesus' name,

AMEN.

Abundant Energy

Be energetic in your life of salvation, reverent
and sensitive before God. That energy
is God's energy, an energy deep within
you, God Himself willing and working at
what will give Him the most pleasure.

PHILIPPIANS 2:12–13, THE MESSAGE

We've heard ourselves say it a million times over:
"I am so exhausted." Just straight-up tired. We
often don't even know why we feel so drained, but
life seems to get the best of us, and before we know it,
we are an empty cup trying our best to pour out what we
don't even have ourselves, unaware that we are bone-dry and
running on empty.

Imagine a solar panel. Its large, flat surface is full of photovoltaic cells,
which are used to absorb solar rays and turn them into electricity or heat
for another source. Don't worry, we won't go into a physics discussion;
hang with me here. The only way these panels can actually do their job is
if they remain out and open, fully exposed to the sunshine to receive what
they need to function.

The same is true for us! Our ability to be able, enthusiastic, joyful, and
grace-giving rests in our attentiveness to the Son. If we do not spend time
with Jesus, taking on His characteristics is impossible. Through striving,
we will do our best, but our human efforts will always leave us and others
depleted and discouraged. We simply cannot attain holiness or lasting happiness outside of our Maker.

However, when we remain in the Son, when we open ourselves up to Him, we soak up His blessings. We realize the abundant supply He has in store for us, and our worry is replaced with peace. This posture provides us with the foundation to pursue His will for our lives, to be sensitive to the Spirit in seeking direction, and to be energetic about this life we live!

The reason and reward for having energy is blessing others with it! If our desire attempts to acquire our own glory, our selfish intent will quickly zap our energy and leave us disappointed. But when we get outside ourselves and we aim our energy at doing good for others for the sake of the gospel, we will tap into the renewable energy source that never runs dry.

Radiating the light of Jesus is not about accumulating enough power to run on our own; it is about depending on Him for our everyday usage and output. Don't we think that if He calls us to something, He wants to give us the energy needed for that task and more? Abundance—that is what He offers as we absorb the goodness of His heart.

Prayer

Hey Jesus, thank You for providing all that I need to carry out all that You ask me to do. When I feel tired or weary, remind me I am depending on my own human effort and lead me back to You. You never lack an abundant power supply. In Jesus' name,

AMEN.

Cultivate the Skills

Do you see a man skillful in his work?
He will stand before kings; he will
not stand before obscure men.

PROVERBS 22:29 ESV

If someone is kind, humble, consistent, loving, and selfless but doesn't have the skills necessary to perform a job, will they be hired for that position? Regardless of what career field we are talking about, the answer is often no. While certain skills can obviously be taught if the spirit of trainability is there, there must be a level of performance that is already intact.

We see this in Scripture time and time again, particularly in the story of David. Though he was a man after God's own heart, it was his skill of playing music that placed him before King Saul. Now we know from reading the Bible that David later replaced Saul as king, but in the meantime David was simply being faithful with the skills he had and making himself available when those skills were needed. Because God knew this, He positioned David in divine ways that took him from a field to a palace in hardly any time at all.

If we want to be God-fearing leaders, we must be willing to do the hard work to learn the skills required for this work. Whatever marketplace we find ourselves in, whatever our roles are at home, or however we spend our days, God gives us the capacity and drive to show up well. As we pursue excellence, others notice. When they ask why we are working so hard or being so "extra," we can explain to them where our motivation comes from and why we are going the extra mile. As children of God, we were never supposed to just "collect a paycheck" or "get by." We were created to flourish.

Whatever it takes—the additional class on a weekend, the extra hours of practice, the sacrifices on our schedule—we must commit to giving our all, even when it's inconvenient. It is not about being the best of all time; it is about putting in the time and trusting God to use us for His best.

However, our ambitious mindset and eagerness to give our all must stem from the desire to make our heavenly Father proud and to depend on Him for what we need. Being a hard worker is fantastic, but if one has the spirit of self-reliance, pride will always be a pitfall. Sooner or later, the desire to stand on a pedestal will be what knocks us to our knees. But when we are dedicated to learning and maintain a teachable spirit, we become unstoppable leaders who cultivate the skills to succeed without compromising our hearts.

Is our relationship with Jesus solely about what we do? No. However, because we yearn to serve Him and reflect His glory, we should be the most capable doers out there.

Prayer

Hey Jesus, thank You for providing all that I need to cultivate the skills in the place I am, for such a time as this. Help me remain humble and dependent on You. I want to pursue excellence so that others will know You are the giver of my success and my stamina. In Jesus' name,

AMEN.

Fruit in the Valley

Consider it pure joy, my brothers and sisters,
whenever you face trials of many kinds,
because you know that the testing of your
faith produces perseverance. Let perseverance
finish its work so that you may be mature
and complete, not lacking anything.

JAMES 1:2-4 NIV

"Mountaintops are views and inspiration but fruit
is grown in the valleys." Billy Graham

We don't want this to be true because we know what it
means for our lives. We wish our lives were all about the
mountaintops—the wide, beautiful views and never about the
valleys—the low, hard stuff that is sometimes painful and all-the-times
difficult. We wish the correct route was an easy path, but the reason it's
honorable is because it's hard. And while we think we'd rather live lives of
comfort and ease, could it be that our souls actually yearn for the fulfillment only found through the difficult?

Mountaintop views are unlike anything we've ever seen. They are unbelievable, making for the best of pictures and memories made. We get to
span the horizon and see the depths of the world below. As we drink in the
view, our bodies feel the scope of the hard work, dedication, commitment,
and faith required to get to the top. All necessary and worth the sacrifice.

We don't wake up dreaming of the valleys. They're hard, pressing, and
full of uncertainty. Sometimes these valleys look like a lost job, a failing
marriage, a miscarriage, struggle with our image, loneliness, or financial
hardship. However it dresses itself, a valley sometimes make us question if
we will get to the other side—will we make it through?

DOES IT GET BETTER?

Somehow, our feet keep moving and we notice the muscles in our legs getting stronger. We stop wishing for change, and we begin praying for perseverance. We begin to cling to hope that we can't yet see, and we learn how deeply our trust is being tested. The moments seem to run together until one day, we are no longer in that valley. The view has changed, new resources are available, and things are different. And then for a split second, we miss the valley. Because somehow, its harshness forced us to rely on the gentleness of our heavenly Father. In the valley, we clung to hope, and it made us bolder in our faith. We never worried about becoming self-reliant there—we needed Jesus with every step.

Whether we are in the valley now or it feels like it is quickly approaching, we remember that the fruit of our faith was forged in our lowest moments. In our weakness, He had to become great within us. The suffering, the struggling—it will still be hard, but it is the very fabric of a life WELL lived and a warrior who is willing to fight.

Look around. Wherever you are, whatever your view, He is doing a new thing in you.

Prayer

Hey Jesus, thank You for the way You use all things, especially the struggles and seasons of hardship. Help me look for Your fingerprints in the valley; I trust You to provide all that I need in each moment. In Jesus' name,

AMEN.

Deal with the Boxes

But you, take courage! Do not let your hands
be weak, for your work shall be rewarded.

II CHRONICLES 15:7 ESV

I knew what he was going to say before I even picked up the phone. My dad was at the storage unit staring at the boxes I had completely avoided going through since I arrived home. After moving back from another city, I had been dreading dealing with sorting through my old belongings, overwhelmed with the uncertainty of my future.

Reluctantly I picked up the phone, and he told me we had twenty-four hours before things had to be completely moved out from that facility. Finally, I went through my old boxes and containers of belongings, and much to my surprise, I found so many things I had been searching for just days prior! There were kitchen supplies I hadn't realized I already owned, shoes I thought I had lost, and some key items I was so happy to discover. I packed up my car and felt the weight leave my shoulders. Something so small and trivial had become a mountain I was avoiding in my head.

How often do we do this? We see the tiniest snowball in our hand, but we let the downfall of dread and the pitfall of procrastination roll it over time and time again, and before we know it, it becomes a boulder of snow we now have to drive around. We avoid situations we know we should deal with, and in doing so, we cause unnecessary stress for ourselves and others.

However, when we decide to push past the discomfort and stop letting our preference determine our level of proactivity, we realize that most of our dread was all in our heads and that our hands were far more capable than we realized. Much like I found the kitchen supplies and shoes I had been searching for, we also will learn that sometimes in our avoidance of dealing with what is in front of us, we don't realize that we already have what we need for what's ahead.

Radiating Jesus isn't always sunshine and rainbows; in fact, often it is putting on the rain boots, finding the umbrella, and dealing with the here and now, even when the forecast feels unpredictable or not preferable. When we do, we will see that Jesus often plants nuggets of wisdom and the greatest of treasures in the most unlikely of places.

Also, let's be honest: There is something to be said for just showing up and doing what we have to do. That, as basic as it sounds, looks a whole lot like Jesus too.

Prayer

Hey Jesus, thank You for giving me the energy and wisdom to show up to do what needs to get done. Help me not avoid the hard stuff and to deal with things head-on so that I can walk into all that You have for me. In Jesus' name,

AMEN.

The Mark of a Warrior

The LORD is my strength and my shield; my heart
trusts in Him, and I am helped; therefore my
heart exults, and with my song I shall thank Him.

PSALM 28:7 NASB

It didn't make any sense. Her cancer had come
back for a second time, as if the first time had
not been terrible enough, stripping her of her
career, her usual routine, and so many of the everyday joys her life had previously included. And now
it was back, and here she was handing me a notebook
full of faith-filled Scriptures for some uncertainties I was
facing. She had taken the time to go through each Scripture
and personally write out my name, along with her scribbled notes
in the margins (which were my favorite) that said things like, "This one
helped me regain strength!" and "This one was my fighting verse."

The scope of what I was potentially facing felt so minuscule compared
to her prognosis, and here she was equipping me with truth to fight my
battle. My friend radiated this warrior-like spirit that was so contagious,
it made everyone want to suit up in jerseys and take the field to go fight.
Though she was dealing with logistics of all kinds and having to make decisions about her future that felt cold and sterile, she brought a warmth into
the atmosphere that was impossible to deny. I would sometimes wonder,
"Would I be angry at God if this was me?" With the way that she served
Him on a daily basis, I found myself wanting to be angry for her, but
how could I question His sovereignty when that thought never crossed her
mind? Or if it did, the truth quickly reminded her of His grace and His
love for her.

My friend told me she had been put in a unique position in which she had no choice but to literally give everything—physically, mentally, emotionally, spiritually—to Jesus. And because of this, she finally understood freedom. We often interpret freedom as being able to do whatever we want, but freedom in Christ is trusting Him to do everything He wants. It is complete and total release of what we thought was our control and the revelation that He longs to satisfy our souls. However, it requires our surrender.

Though my friend lost her battle with cancer, she did not lose the battle that counts. Her perfect healing was in heaven, but her life on earth reminded all those watching what it means to be a true warrior in our faith. The veil between heaven and earth had become thin, and she lived her life reminding others that even in our suffering, God is good and He is so near.

May we also fight well. Let's live our lives radiating our hope of heaven and our trust in His plans.

Prayer

Hey Jesus, thank You for the way You equip me to fight the good fight of faith. Whatever my lot, You are with me. Help me praise You and trust You to always deliver in Your perfect way, whatever that means for me. In Jesus' name,

AMEN.

The Real Deal

> Do not be conformed to this world, but be transformed by the renewal of your mind, that by testing you may discern what is the will of God, what is good and acceptable and perfect.
>
> ROMANS 12:2 ESV

When we search for reviews online, we expect those who have gone to a particular restaurant, store, or place we are considering going to be honest and helpful in their feedback. We want firsthand knowledge of what it will be like before we personally experience it so that we can decide beforehand if it's worth it. We want to know the best dishes, what the atmosphere is like, and if the customer service will earn our generous tip.

Though it sounds silly, this is often very similar to our faith. The world is constantly searching and watching, even if subconsciously, for the "trick" to having a full life. They have heard of this "Jesus" guy—they want to know if He is the real deal. They want to know if prayers are actually heard and if Christians are truly kind and loving people outside the confines of their carefully constructed social circles. For lack of better terms, their craving for an abundant life finds them entering this question into the search bar: "Is Jesus who He says He is, and is being a Christian all it's cracked up to be?"

The thing about it is this: God does not have to compete against a negative experience or any action we don't understand on this side of heaven; He is superior to all. God is actually who He says He is. Life with Him is actually as He describes it. His Word is completely true. However, much like our desire to see pictures of a dish before we order it, those around us are looking at our lives—the character we exhibit, the works of our hands, and the way we handle stress—and they want to know what a Christ-follower's life actually looks like. Is it worth the sacrifice?

We already know this to be true; it's the reason we break our backs trying to appear perfect. However, the world is not looking for us to be Jesus; they are looking for us to live as if we are loved by Him. They don't need another fake example of a filtered life; they need an authentic example of a vulnerable, peace-filled life.

Does our speech sound different from that of those who don't believe? Are we quick to get angry or spread gossip? When we leave our worship experience on Sunday, is the car ride home filled with bitterness and unrest? Do we stop to see and serve others around us, even when it's inconvenient?

At any moment, we are either reflecting the heart of the Father or giving in to fear. Even the moments that seem trivial are opportunities to radiate the hope of Jesus. When we live with joy, depend on prayer, and choose the way of peace, we are writing reviews for our heavenly Father that others get to read. As we seek Him, they see Him in us.

May our prayers, praise, and posture point to a perfect, unshakable God.

Prayer

Hey Jesus, thank You for Your consistent nature. I depend on Your unchanging love and grace. Keep praise on my lips today; I want to be a person of gratitude. Remind me of the power of each moment and conversation as I speak of Your name. In Jesus' name,

AMEN.

Playing Dress-Up

Therefore, as God's chosen people, holy and
dearly loved, clothe yourselves with compassion,
kindness, humility, gentleness and patience.

COLOSSIANS 3:12 NIV

What if we are thinking of our identity in the
complete opposite way of how God intended?
Instead of thinking that we must add to ourselves
or strive to be someone He would approve of, we
must realize that beneath the layers of who we think
we should be, the raw version of us looks more like
Jesus. In other words, we have all that we need to look like
Him in and of ourselves, and as we spend time with Him,
we begin to reflect His image. Sanctification (the process of being
made holy) removes what we "put on" to measure up and refines us in
His image.

Imagine it as dress-up. Roll with me here for a moment; let me explain
the analogy. We think we are dressed in one outfit, seeking to impress and
become and achieve to be labeled as one way. However, in reality, it is
when we remove the wardrobe of the world and our souls are refined by
our Maker that the real us comes forth. Faith requires works, yes. However, those works are not about acquiring what we don't have or becoming
someone we are not; they are in the direction of chiseling away what is
distracting and defeating us from realizing we are already heirs of Christ.

Radiating is our God-given right when our eyes are opened to His reflection in us and through us! It is not an achievement gained through striving
but a revelation of living out of our God-given identity that was established
for us on the cross. When God made the birds and the trees and the stars

and the seas, He said it was all good. However, it was only when He created humankind that He molded us in His likeness. He crafted us with the intention of reflecting Him. And when sin entered the world, Jesus took our sin and our shame and lavished His grace on us to be our covering. This means that earning our identity has never been possible; we can only receive the gift that has already been given to us and live out of this truth.

What costumes do we find ourselves trying to "put on" in order to seem better or more qualified for such a gift? Do we try to add spiritual jargon or accolades to our board, hoping it will solidify our place?

May we take a deep breath and find rest in knowing that our identity was sealed by Jesus, not sanctioned by us. As we uncover the depths of amazing grace, we will stop trying to "dress up" in a way to impress others or God and instead spend our lives lying bare before Him, fully aware that not a morsel of heavenly hope can be earned. Made in His image, identified as His children, all because of love.

Prayer

Hey Jesus, thank You for Your amazing grace that crafted us in Your image. When we feel tempted to "put on" anything to impress You or the world, remind us that we have all that we need to radiate You. Made in Your image, oh what love! In Jesus' name,

AMEN.

If you are not royalty,
He is not King.

BETH MOORE

Keep Turning the Pages

God saved us and called us to live a holy life. He
did this, not because we deserved it, but because
that was His plan from before the beginning of
time—to show us His grace through Christ Jesus.

II TIMOTHY 1:9 NLT

We know it to be true in the books that we read,
in the movies that we watch, and in most things
that we intake—more is ahead. When one chapter
feels incredibly heavy, we trust that resolution and
peace will be in the pages that follow. It allows us to keep
our heads up and our eyes open to stay engaged and keep
reading because we have seen the pattern time and time again:
this is not the end.

However, when it comes to our own story, it feels way harder to place faith
in anything other than what we are currently experiencing. The chapter
we are on or the one we are about to start burdens our chest and makes
our feet wobbly, and we just want to get past it. Sometimes, these seasons
are even traumatic, laced with deep grief, fear, and incomprehensible pain.
Jesus never said we would be spared from such. And though sometimes we
wish it, we can't fast-forward through the parts of our story that feel like
they don't belong.

What can we do though? We can survey what every other tough moment
or tough season has done for us—it has made us tougher. Tougher in spirit,
tenacity, strength, and courage, while simultaneously making us more tender to the heart of God, ourselves, and those around us. Our best efforts
to empathize would be minuscule if we had not traveled through difficult
waters ourselves. These times furnish in us a compassion that can only be
built, not bought.

The truth of our story is this: If we keep turning the pages, putting one foot in front of the other, we will walk to the other side and our perspective will be heightened. The perpetual sunrise and sunset keep our minds steadfast as we remember that the Creator of our lives and the Author of our faith has purpose in all He brings to pass. Wherever we are right now, we can cling to this truth and know that Jesus really does use everything for our good.

We were never supposed to make sense of all the parts of our story or comprehend the why; the very essence of our faith and the point of our lives is developing an unwavering, unbridled, unshakable trust in Jesus. It is all about the who. And guess what? His fingerprints are on every page, especially the ones we tend to wish away. Chapters later, we will see how each part, each person, and each prayer—answered and unanswered—was pivotal in order to radiate the One holding the pen.

Prayer

Hey Jesus, thank You for the way You use every moment of my life to show me Your sovereignty, power, and kindness. When my heart is weary or afraid, reaffirm my trust in Your plan. Give me the strength to turn the next page. In Jesus' name,

AMEN.

God-Conscious

I will give them a heart to know Me, for I
am the LORD; and they will be My people,
and I will be their God, for they will
return to Me with their whole heart.

JEREMIAH 24:7 NASB

We don't mean to make us the center. It just
happens. It's so easy to follow the lies that we can
achieve happiness on our own as long as we follow
our hearts. And where does this leave us? Frustrated,
tired from all the striving, and confused about what He
wants from us. We have become so self-focused, and yet
nothing we do keeps us from feeling self-conscious.

But that's exactly how we become the center of our lives—we don't
"mean to." Our nature is always going to be self-focused, even in the way
we pursue God. Our efforts are often seen through the lens of self-righ-
teousness or self-approval; we think if we can do enough, we will become
what would make God proud. But when we are intentional about redirect-
ing our focus from the creation to the Creator, everything shifts.

Instead of operating FOR fulfillment, we operate out of fulfillment.

Instead of chasing accolades, we cling to the approval already established
for us. We are no longer tossed to and fro by the winds of culture or the
fear of people.

Instead of keeping our eyes peeled for the next best thing that we think
might bring us happiness, we know we can go to His well—at any moment,
every day, no matter how we are dressed or if we messed up. We can drink.

Rest. Gather our energy. It's the only place we can go to quench the thirst deep within us.

When we are self-conscious, we have such a heightened awareness of our frailty and our false hope; instead of drawing us to Him, our pride convinces us to keep trying. It leaves us ragged and discontent. But when we are God-conscious, the revelation of our frailty becomes the door to gratitude and we radiate reverence of Him. Wisdom opens our eyes to His amazing grace, showing us the reality of our humanity that now receives the unshakable covering of Jesus. This is our true hope. We see that we don't have to be enough because He is our everything.

We don't have to constantly look in the mirror and evaluate whether we are worthy, capable, or victorious. We have the gift of looking at Jesus, the One who goes before us in everything, and recentering our awareness on His worthiness, His capability, and His victory. We were never meant to be the center of our lives. Only He can handle the pressure, navigate the path, and usher in the peace we need to live a rich, full life.

It seems obvious that we would pick being God-conscious over being self-conscious, and yet we live so much of our lives picking the latter. But today, we get to decide again—so what will it be?

Prayer

Hey Jesus, thank You for the reminder that when we focus on You, You bring all things into correct perspective. Rid myself of me. I know that when I recenter all around You, peace and fulfillment become mine. In Jesus' name,

AMEN.

Shining amid Disappointment

*Trust in him at all times, O people; pour out
your heart before him; God is a refuge for us.*

PSALM 62:8 ESV

We all know what it feels like: the sting of disappointment when things don't go as we hoped or when our prayers seem to be falling on deaf ears. We begin to question if God hears us. Or, rather, does He care? We think to ourselves, "He is God. He is King over everything, so why won't He change my situation?"

God is okay with that. He knows the reality we are facing and that our spirits are bruised. He reminds us that even the Son of God, the Messiah, Jesus, felt this sting. Before Jesus went to be crucified, He knew the impending circumstances were going to be harder than anything He had ever faced. He was to take the weight of the world on His shoulders, and He felt the human emotions that we feel. But there was a striking difference with Jesus that we all can learn from. As He went off alone to pray, He told God, "Father, if You are willing, please take this cup of suffering away from Me. Yet I want Your will to be done, not Mine" (Luke 22:42 NLT).

How often do we feel like Jesus, but with far less intense circumstances and pressure? We pray and plea for God to pull the "God card." Doesn't He see what we are enduring? We begin to bargain with Him, hoping that if we agree to serving Him with our lives, He will just fix this situation, this relationship, this hardship.

However, we see that Jesus continued to walk up the hill to be crucified. The second part of Jesus' prayer is the revealing of His heart: "I want Your will to be done, not Mine." He knew that His human flesh temporarily wanted relief, but His deepest desire was to please His Father.

Jesus' trust was fully in His heavenly Father, but that did not change the breaking, the hurt, the disappointment, or the suffering He endured. He knew the burden of unanswered prayer, of desperately desiring a different outcome than the one He would receive. And yet, He remained in His Father's will, confident that if God was bringing something to pass, it was necessary for peace.

May we remember this: Jesus' greatest display of radiance and love for His heavenly Father was the act from which His flesh most wanted to be removed. Because He remained obedient, even when the outcome was not what He hoped, He became the Light of the world. And now we have the same opportunity—to trust the heart of God, even when we are disappointed or afraid. He will only give us His best.

Prayer

Hey Jesus, thank You for being the ultimate example of shining in the midst of disappointment. Help me remember I can trust You, even when relief feels far away. Your will is always the richest pathway to life—I choose it. In Jesus' name,

AMEN.

A Million Little Ways

Be on your guard; stand firm in the faith; be courageous; be strong.

I CORINTHIANS 16:13 NIV

When we think about courage, we often imagine major acts of valor. We have seen the movies where the hero saves the people from the villain; we have read stories about soldiers going to war, historical figures taking a stand for justice, and people fighting on behalf of the under-dog. These grandiose acts of bravery often set us up to assume that to be courageous, we have to do something wild or big, right?

However, courage is carried out most frequently in the smallest of ways. When we choose to show up and have that hard conversation, when we stop and speak to the man on the corner, or when we apply to that pro-gram we have been thinking about joining—it can be anything. These moments, big and small, require us to push past what we currently see or have in our hands and believe for something greater. It is in these seem-ingly mundane acts that our perseverance is built and our hope is required to push through to help us walk to the other side. Courage is the actionable intel of faith—when we take steps of faith, it verifies that we truly believe.

Sometimes, I think we focus on the big things we don't think we can reach for instead of stepping forward into the small things that are within our grasp. It's almost as if the "reach for the stars" mentality handicaps us into believing that if the act doesn't change the world or shift our lives com-pletely, it isn't courage at all. This crafty little lie is straight from the king liar himself. The enemy wants us to be paralyzed by possibility instead of being propelled by progress. He is fully aware of what will happen if we begin to take the small steps, one after the other after the other: we will realize that the big thing is not so far away after all.

Courage is not always manifested through a large, specific something; rather, it is developed through a million little ways. Because here's the thing Jesus wants us to get about courage: It was never about the thing we thought it was. It was about the transfer of trust that took place as we took one step after another. The little ways were the big ways because the transformation was the point.

Prayer

Hey Jesus, thank You for giving me a spirit of courage and perseverance. Help me see challenges as opportunities to practice my faith and be bold. I want to say yes wherever You ask me to follow. In Jesus' name,

AMEN.

Valuable Vessels

Do you not know that your body is a temple of the Holy Spirit who is in you, whom you have from God, and that you are not your own?

I CORINTHIANS 6:19 NASB

I've always struggled with my self-image. If it's not my weight, it's my skin. If it's not my skin, it's something else. Unfortunately, I think we all struggle with body image or self-acceptance in one way or another. Male and female, young and old, whoever we are and however we were raised, there are imperfections we all become painfully aware of the longer we live.

I've heard before that the enemy likes to work in our minds in this area like a boxer's cut: He hits us where we have a scar from a previous wound, knowing the tenderness and vulnerability we will feel when hit in that specific place. He takes a jab at just the right spot, hoping the old wound will reopen and we will once again be nursing the same place that took us down last time. Sometimes these jabs from the enemy come through the lens of comparison, the critical self-talk we allow to snowball, the gossip we overhear, or the societal standard set by unrealistic expectations and inaccurate definitions of who we are supposed to be and what we are supposed to look like. We know that a blow from just one of these can sometimes send us to our knees, but they draw us in through disguising themselves as "no big deal" or "everyone goes through it."

The truth of the Word of God calls out a different reality for us here: We are set apart. Our bodies are called to be temples of the Most High God. This is not an analogy for the sake of illustration; He actually lives inside of us, continually transforming us from the inside out. When He watches us take the jab and forget we have the defense of truth on our side, His heart breaks. An offense to His child is an offense to Him; that is how much He values us!

So may I ask—what lies are you believing about yourself right now that don't deserve the attention and focus you are giving them? What does Jesus say about you that you need to remind yourself of today so that you can radiate the worthiness of your Maker?

Our brokenness, frailty, and weakness are not deterrents for Him; they are the entire reason He came. It's time we all came to the realization that how we see ourselves is a direct reflection of how we view our heavenly Father. If He chose to take up residence in us, then how we value ourselves is directly equivalent to how much we value Him.

Prayer

Hey Jesus, thank You for crafting me, refining me, purifying me, and claiming me. Help me see myself, specifically my physical body, as You see it. Pure, whole, capable—a vessel for Your purpose, perfect in You. In Jesus' name,

AMEN.

Longing for Belonging

We grew up doing it. Remember the games or
"tests" where a series of cards, blocks, or figu-
rines were presented and we were told to find
the one that didn't belong in the group? There
was something similar about all the components
except one little lone ranger. Noticing the outlier and
pulling it out of the haystack ensured our success and
solidified our intelligence, right (well, as much as something like that can)?

The thing is, I think a lot of times we feel like someone is about to pick
us out of the stack and tell us we are the one that doesn't belong. Even
when we have been in a friend group for years, new seasons bring new
transitions, mindsets, thoughts, and relationships. While we welcome these
changes as we ourselves are walking through them, we wonder if those
around us will suddenly decide that we are the card that doesn't match
with the rest of the deck. Because God wove belonging into the fabric of
our hearts, it would make sense that it's one of the first ways the enemy
tries to discourage us.

However, there is a truth that sets us free: Because God dreamed us up,
molded us, and claimed us, there is never a moment in which He would
deny that we are part of His family. Because our identity is not tied to our
performance, our worst behavior cannot negate the Father's love for us.
But it is in the revelation of being forever included that we extend this same

warm invitation to others—no preconceived notions, judgment, or bylaws that should change whether they belong.

As believers, we should be the most inclusive, kind, welcoming, tender, and loving people in the world. It is because of the grace we have been extended and the scars on our Savior's hands that we even get the opportunity to reach out our own hands. We read about our King sitting with tax collectors, forgiving the worst sinners, and pursuing the rejected. If we believe all this to be true, who are we to set different standards?

We all have the unashamed, forever stamp of the Creator. When our anxiety starts to reel about whether we belong, may we go back to this truth. When our flesh flares up and tries to exclude someone due to race, social status, cultural background, career choice, or whatever it may be, we must revert to this truth. We were woven with the desire to belong—a longing for belonging. It is the very thing that draws us back to Jesus, who welcomes us into His lasting embrace.

Prayer

Hey Jesus, thank You for the way You affirm my spirit through claiming me as Yours. I know Your love is all-inclusive; help me give love in the same way. Show me how to build a longer table, not a taller fence. In Jesus' name,

AMEN.

PSA: Drink Water

Whoever believes in me, as the Scripture has said,
"Out of his heart will flow rivers of living water."

JOHN 7:38 ESV

When we are thirsty, being in the heat is rough. In the South come mid-July, it gets so incredibly hot and humid that a shower is useless. The minute you step outside, your hair gets sweaty. In the heat, dehydration can happen quickly, as we are often unaware of the root of our discomfort and pain until we are forced to find a remedy. We continue to power along until the headache from the dehydration becomes overwhelming and we are forced to seek what we needed all along: water.

In North America, we are blessed to have water readily available to us, no matter our socioeconomic status. We have travel cups for days, bottles of water thrown in our cars, and refrigerators full of water, and yet we still manage to forget to take in the most essential ingredient to our survival, other than Jesus. Why do you think that is? Usually, when something is so readily available and abundantly so, we tend to forget its importance and take it for granted. That is, until that headache comes along, signaling to us we are off-kilter and in need of a refill.

I believe we do this in our spiritual lives as well. We know that the most vital, life-giving, and useful thing we can do is spend time with Jesus, and yet it often requires a terrible day, an emotional breakdown, or a full stress attack to remind us of this importance. Because His grace is so available and because we know the faithfulness of His character, we let His well be the last place we go, even though we know it is always the place that saves us. But what if the well became the first place we go to, the space that protects us and prepares us for the journey ahead, instead of the place we turn to only after we finally realize we are thirsty?

As we come to Jesus, we are filled and our thirst is quenched. It is then, and only then, that we can be of service to others. Out of our hearts will flow rivers of living water supplied by the Holy Spirit. In other words, when we drink of the goodness of Jesus, we will always have overflow. As our hearts are purified as we sit with Him, we become helpers who point to the well and offer a drink of water to others on the way.

The journey of life will sometimes feel long, exhausting, and hot, but we have received the energy and sustenance we need to get to the other side.

Prayer

Hey Jesus, thank You for the eternal invite to come to Your well, drink of Your goodness, and be thirsty no more. You satisfy my soul. Anchor my heart in Yours so that I can be a river of living water to those around me. In Jesus' name,

AMEN.

Please Don't Be Polite

Whoever conceals their sins does not prosper, but the one who confesses and renounces them finds mercy.

PROVERBS 28:13 NIV

Honestly, I didn't expect it to even come out. It had been quite the week—you know, the kind of week where you feel like you can't catch a break. I had to have a few hard conversations, taxes were coming up, and upon getting my oil changed, I learned that three of my four tires needed to be replaced. Mind you, finances were already at the top of my worry list that month. How was all of this happening at the same time?

However, my issues felt so small and so trivial compared to those experienced by people who are struggling to put food on the table or make ends meet. Voicing my needs to others felt selfish and childish, and so I didn't. That is, until my friend asked me at the gym, "So, how have things been?" Cue volcanic eruption of emotion. I let everything come to the surface and bubble over.

They expected my polite answer of "Pretty good but busy!" which I managed to give them, followed by the full-on waterworks accompanied by my real answer, which I did not expect to hand out that day. In trying to be courteous to everyone else, I had become a danger to myself, isolating my own mind from those who could call me out in truth. As soon as I let the words flow and another set of shoulders was carrying the weight I had been feeling, two major things happened.

One was that in the power of confession, I could hear the enemy behind my fears. Giving light to what I was keeping inside finally allowed me to see it for what it really was: fear, not truth. The gates of my own personal prison burst wide open, and surprisingly enough, I was still standing and stronger for it.

Two, giving breath to this space I felt locked in meant that I was no longer the only one who lived there. Inviting someone else into my struggle and my current mindset dispelled the power of isolation. I had never actually been alone (shout-out to Jesus), but to know that I now had someone who could ask me the hard questions, keep me accountable, and pray for me— it meant everything. Community is necessary at all times, but it is a lifeline in hard times.

Had I known the tears were going to fall and the truth was going to come out that day at the gym, I probably would've avoided my friend like the plague. But, Jesus. He knew that I needed someone in the flesh to remind me that sharing our hearts does not weigh others down; it gives us the opportunity to join hands in lifting each other up.

Don't be afraid to let someone else know what's really going on—it might just be what they need too.

Prayer

Hey Jesus, thank You for the gift of Christ-centered community. When I find myself feeling alone, unimportant, or unseen, help me seek out another. Thank You for the reminder that our need doesn't make us weak; it makes us human, and You are good with that. In Jesus' name,

AMEN.

Better Than the Reviews

This is eternal life, that they may know You, the only true God, and Jesus Christ whom You have sent.

JOHN 17:3 NASB

My husband and I got married in Isla Mujeres, Mexico. This small hidden gem is only a short ferry ride away from Cancún, and it is a dream. There are hardly any cars on the island because it's so small that most natives and tourists ride mopeds or golf carts.

My mom and I went for a week to plan the wedding and meet all the vendors, and it was magical. We became fast friends with the locals, learned about all the fun places, found the best "hole-in-the-wall" spot for guacamole, and discovered the magic of the island in the most unlikely of places.

As our family and friends made all their reservations, I tried to explain the island to them, but it felt impossible. The online pictures didn't do it justice, and the best restaurants weren't included in any online search! Though I attempted to help them visualize the beauty, it was not until everyone arrived and experienced the island that they saw it for themselves. My emails now came alive as they navigated around the island, met the locals, and learned quickly that some places just can't be captured in words.

Many had read articles, looked Isla up on Instagram, and googled it in every capacity, but they only learned about Isla. They did not know Isla. There is a major difference.

Sometimes I think we are the same way with Jesus without even realizing it. We spend so much time learning about what a relationship with Him looks like, we read Christian books, and we go to church and hear about the power of prayer. But knowing about Jesus and knowing Jesus are two very different things. Knowing about Jesus provides knowledge, but it is only in the knowing of Jesus that we are able to apply that wisdom and have a real relationship with Him.

Jesus, even in His own words, cannot be summed up. We can believe something has great value, but until we decide it is worth the cost in our own personal lives, we remain standing on the perimeter. When we get to know Jesus, we will not want to stop getting to know Him, which is a journey that will last until we meet Him face-to-face. His grace will become apparent, we will feel His tenderness as we speak, and He will no longer feel so distant in our hearts. As we draw near, so does He. Our prayers, posture, and promises turn from airy to absolute as we realize that He is one million times better than the best explanation we could ever read about Him.

Prayer

Hey Jesus, thank You for the way You draw near as we pursue You. Help me concern myself with not just knowing about You but rather knowing You. In Jesus' name,

AMEN.

You Won't Miss It

But seek first the kingdom of God and his righteousness, and all these things will be added to you. Therefore do not be anxious about tomorrow, for tomorrow will be anxious for itself. Sufficient for the day is its own trouble.

MATTHEW 6:33–34 ESV

I couldn't stop going back to this question no matter how hard I tried. Nothing crazy had happened that day, or that week for that matter, but it kept circling in my thoughts and bringing me anxiety despite my best attempts to keep it at bay.

"What if I miss it?"

That was the question, the constant nagging at my spirit, and I couldn't shut it up, run away from it, or pretend I didn't hear it. I was afraid that I was going to miss what God had for my life. Once I allowed that emotion to take root, it built a spiderweb in my head and convinced me that I didn't have the ability to hear God and that the voice that had gotten me to where I was that day was simply my own murmuring.

Can you relate at all? The holy desire to live a life of purpose and leave a legacy rich in Jesus is a wonderful thing, but when we let the enemy convince us that our pride or our own self-reliance has the power to override God's purpose for us, we are missing it! Not missing our purpose, but missing the point!

I will never forget when I was crying out to God one day after making a huge change in my life and He reminded me: "Cleere, I am big and mighty enough to get you exactly where I want you to go. Remember who I am."

That was it. Sometimes I think we confuse what God values, believing He values the outcome of our obedience over our obedience. The truth is, He never needs us. He uses us, guides us, and redeems us for His glory, but our story is never required to turn something wrong into something right. He can wave His hand and change everything. He treasures our obedience because it reveals our trust, and our trust reveals how we see Him. When we believe the lie that we could miss His plan for us when we are pursuing Him, we are seeing ourselves as too big and Him as too small.

The quickest way to snap out of a mindset like this is to recenter our focus on truth: Who is He? Then, in turn, who are we because of who He is? When we continually reposition ourselves as His children and remember that He is a good heavenly Father, our souls find comfort in knowing we don't serve a God who lets us miss it. Because of Him, we get to radiate purpose.

He has us. Onward we go, pursuing holiness and integrity while accepting His grace and trusting that He will always lead us in the way of righteousness.

Prayer

Hey Jesus, thank You for the reminder of how big, mighty, and capable You are. It is my remembrance of You that gives me confidence and peace in where I am. Hold me close and remind my heart that You will never let me miss what You have for me when I am pursuing You. In Jesus' name,

AMEN.

If you are a
Christian, your
search for approval
should be over.

DAVID JEREMIAH

Forget Yourself

> I have been crucified with Christ. It is no longer
> I who live, but Christ who lives in me. And the
> life I now live in the flesh I live by faith in the Son
> of God, who loved me and gave himself for me.

GALATIANS 2:20 ESV

Do you have a fear of public speaking? Or what is something that makes you terribly nervous to do in front of others?

The first time I spoke at a conference, someone gave me the most incredible advice. She told me to go look in the mirror, take one last good look, and then forget myself.

At first, I wasn't fully sure what she meant until the time came for me to speak. Nauseous and nervous, I went to the bathroom after they adjusted my headset mic. I parted my hair, smiled, and truly said out loud, "Lord, now help me forget me." It wasn't like a magic carpet whisked me away or anything in the atmosphere changed, but it was as if by voicing that simple prayer out loud, a new authority took over.

The mission at hand had nothing to do with me personally. Jesus had deposited something in me to share, and He needed me to actually be able to see the women I would be talking to—*really* see them. But in order to do that, I had to get past myself and how they viewed me. My lens was no longer about their facial expressions based on my words but about their heart posture toward the Lord and His Word. In remembering my why and surrendering to my who, I was able to forget myself and take my mission seriously.

That's the thing about fear, insecurity, and timidity: It keeps our eyes on us, which dramatically limits the impact of what God wants to do through us. We begin to have tunnel vision, only seeing how situations can elevate or diminish us rather than what they can do for the kingdom. In our desire to control the perceptions of others, we aren't able to fully love them because we are too consumed with how they see us to truly see them.

Healthy people see others, forgetting themselves and focusing on the mission at hand. This doesn't mean perfection or full selflessness is attained; rather, it becomes clear that the most important thing is pointing to Jesus.

And you know what is cool and crazy and so like Jesus? When we forget ourselves, He takes lavish care of us. He honors our sacrifice, preserves our purity, protects our peace, and safeguards our image. Why? Because in forgetting ourselves, we look so much like Him.

Prayer

Hey Jesus, thank You for still loving me, even when I choose to put myself first. Help me deny my flesh and the glitter it attracts. Make me mission minded, hungry to do Your will and radiate Your image. In Jesus' name,

AMEN.

Life in 3D

It is the Spirit who gives life; the flesh
profits nothing; the words that I have
spoken to you are spirit and are life.

JOHN 6:63 NASB

Have you ever gone to a 3D movie? It's such a
wild experience. Whether it be *The Avengers* or
Despicable Me, the movie comes alive as you put
on the glasses. The characters now feel like your
friends, the places feel like they're around you, and
when someone flies, you feel like you are in the sky
with them.

I remember wondering what it was about the glasses that actually allows this experience to take place. Come to find out, during a 3D movie, our brain is creating a picture from two different two-dimensional pictures. During filming, the camera has a red lens and a cyan blue lens shooting from the same angle but producing different images. This is where the glasses come in—in order for those two images to make sense and be combined, the red-cyan glasses have to be worn so that the eyes can be directed as to what to see. It is the filter of these colors and our new perspective that makes the movie come alive so that we can fly with Superman, walk through the forest with the avatars, and feel like we have truly been in these movies.

I wonder how many of us are walking around this earth without our glasses on, aka the Holy Spirit, so the picture still looks flat. While we can understand the story line and digest the knowledge of what is happening, our interaction is very much limited and there is still distance between us and what God is doing around us. Unlike a 3D movie, though, the Holy

Spirit is not a fictional way to pretend we see the hand of God working; He is living and active inside of us so that we can finally see the world in color.

When we allow Him to take up residence inside of us and our spiritual glasses are on, things that were once flat, ordinary, or far away become tangible, alive, and extraordinary.

Close your eyes and picture yourself in a movie theater so you can get a visual: The fruit of the Spirit is a jar we can reach into and grab what we need. Prayer is a stairway that we can walk up and see our circumstances from heaven's view. The darts from the enemy are fought off with our shield of faith (Avengers style, of course).

It sounds cheesy, but it's because we sometimes believe the lie that our faith is to be learned, not experienced. But Jesus gave us an eternal pair of glasses when He gave us the Holy Spirit. Life was never meant to be stale, boring, or flat. Maybe it's just time to ask ourselves: are we participating in life or watching it pass us by without seeing its beauty and fullness?

Prayer

Hey Jesus, thank You for the gift of the Holy Spirit so that I get to participate in Your miracles on a daily basis! Help me see from Your perspective. You bring life and color to even the most mundane of places or days. In Jesus' name,

AMEN.

Cross the Bridge

On the glorious splendor of Your majesty and
on Your wonderful works, I will meditate.

PSALM 145:5 NASB

My hometown is only about an hour and fifteen minutes from the beach, so we often spend weekends there throughout the year. Growing up, I did not realize the importance of this place to my soul, but now as an adult, I find myself craving the salt air. There is something that happens when my tires hit the bridge that takes me to the beach; it's as though my worries don't have an access pass to the beach and I can leave them behind me. As I watch the boats cross underneath the bridge, the American flags waving in the air on the light poles, and the ocean crashing beneath me, I take a deep, deep breath, as if the air is new again.

Nothing changes and yet everything does. It's as though this bridge reminds me of how we should travel through life—holding lightly to all we've known because better and more beautiful things are up ahead. The farther we get along the bridge, or the more spiritual maturity we gain, the more we can see life from heaven's perspective. This supernatural vision allows us to experience the beauty in the present but not place our security in the temporary.

Sometimes when the world is pressing down on my shoulders and the weight feels like too much to bear, I want to just drive my car and roll down my windows and smell the salt air. It's as though traveling toward the majesty of the ocean makes me remember how small I am and how big God is. The emails don't fade, the workload is still there, and the obligations are not erased, but my posture becomes one of joy and great anticipation, knowing that tomorrow will come but for now I only have to focus on today.

How can we "cross the bridge" in our everyday lives? Is there a space in our homes, at a local park, or somewhere that we can go that reminds us to rest in His majesty and remember His splendor? What helps us find our deep breath and triggers our prayer life? May we be intentional with cultivating whatever routine is necessary to be in step with the rhythm of grace.

While salt air is a helpful additive, our deep breath can always be found in the eternal perspective of heaven. God is near and He is faithful. Let's rest in that.

Prayer

Hey Jesus, thank You for the unique and beautiful ways that You remind us of Your majesty and splendor. Your unchanging faithfulness is the foundation for my peace. Help me "cross the bridge" no matter what place I lay my head. In Jesus' name,

AMEN.

The In-Between

Rather, you must grow in the grace
and knowledge of our LORD and
Savior Jesus Christ. All glory to Him,
both now and forever! Amen.

II PETER 3:18 NLT

When we know what we are looking for, expect
the outcome we hope to receive, or have a very
clear destination in mind, it is much easier to stay
motivated and inspired to keep going. It allows us
to paint a picture in our minds of what we will soon
be experiencing, and therefore we are able to endure the
process and the space in-between.

Aimlessness is a tactic that the enemy loves to throw at us; he hopes
that we will become discouraged by our current view and wonder if we are
truly making a difference. He knows that when our focus turns to whether
we are doing it right, our eyes are off Jesus and our goal becomes our own
self- advancement or self-glorification. While this is certainly a human tendency, it's not what God intended for us.

God's priority is our depending on His presence because He knows our
joy—His joy—is found through the intimacy of us being together. Unlike
us, He knows the end from the beginning, so the in-between time of what
we do on earth does not plague His mind with worry or paralyze Him with
fear. We often get so fixated on what we hope to do or who we hope to
become that the desire to have a holy purpose itself becomes an idol. How
oxymoronic is that!

How do we radiate a life of purpose without obsessing about where we are going? We trust Him with the details, the detours, and the disappointments. If we think we want to live a big life that serves the kingdom, how much more do you think He wants it for us?

The journey of life isn't always comfortable: transition lurks at every corner, tragedies happen, and transformation is not a one-and-done kind of process. Our purpose is the working out of our salvation so that we can become more like Jesus. The hard part? Believing that He can use every part of the journey for our good, trusting that He is present even when He's silent, and continuing to walk when the road signs are fuzzy in the distance.

Interlocked fingers with the Creator of the stars—that is our purpose. It all goes back to that.

Prayer

Hey Jesus, thank You for the way You meet me every step of my journey. Help me find my purpose in knowing You, even when I feel aimless in what I am doing. I know You will use it all. In Jesus' name,

AMEN.

You Hit a Wall

Behold, I will bring to it health and healing,
and I will heal them; and I will reveal to
them an abundance of peace and truth.

JEREMIAH 33:6 NASB

It is humbling to realize how often we pursue perfection over wholeness, self-reliance over dependence, and control over surrender. It is as though we run up against the same wall, just painted a different color. We start after it, desiring something different, but the closer we get to it, we see that we are once again at the end of ourselves.

Somehow, amid the stories we have been told as children, the articles we have read as adults, and everything we have experienced in between, we have believed the lie that radiating the Spirit of Jesus is equivalent to being Jesus. However, living to look like someone is a far cry from trying to become that person. Jesus is the only embodied perfection earth will ever know, and yet we spend so many waking hours striving after our human interpretation of what perfection looks like. Is it someone without blemish and a past without a mistake? Though impossible, even this definition is not what satisfies a longing heart.

Our hearts believe they want to get rid of the imperfections, but in actuality, they are yearning for communion with perfection itself. This is the path to wholeness—experiencing communion with God. When we have the deep-seated revelation that wholeness is the point, the journey becomes far less about what we lack and way more about what He fills. This change of focus helps shift our minds from a self-defeating mindset to a grace-filled perspective. We see Him start to fill all the spaces that we never could and worship becomes our posture.

When we attempt to run after perfection, we are essentially trying to replace Jesus, because perfect people don't need a Savior. Because it's impossible, we end up discouraged by the battle and ashamed at our motive in fighting. But wholeness lets the light in. Wholeness acknowledges that completion and fullness require a Savior *and* require our brokenness. We are an essential part of the piece! The very humanity we want to wish away is our golden ticket to His gates—a gift!

We can let our shoulders rest today, breathe a little deeper, and slow down our heart rate. We are not here to save the world; we are here to accept the redemption of the One who has already saved it and spend our lives telling others how it happened.

When we get to this wall again, we must have help from the Almighty to scale it, bulldoze it, or seek a different direction. We need Him and that is okay. It's more than okay—it's holy reliance, and it is our source of life.

Prayer

Hey Jesus, thank You for reminding me that You don't want me to be perfect; You want me to be whole. Help me see that I desperately need a Savior and help me live responding to such grace. In Jesus' name,

AMEN.

Recalibrate, Refocus, Reset

Therefore, since we are surrounded by so great
a cloud of witnesses, let us also lay aside every
weight, and sin which clings so closely, and let us
run with endurance the race that is set before
us, looking to Jesus, the founder and perfecter
of our faith, who for the joy that was set before
him endured the cross, despising the shame, and
is seated at the right hand of the throne of God.

HEBREWS 12:1-2 ESV

So often we get in these patterns of fixing our eyes on
what we can see, hold, or fix and our anxiety starts to spin.

Our energy feels zapped.
Our resources feel strapped.
And looking around, we feel lapped.

We feel as though those around us are running the way we wish we could
and now we have convinced ourselves we are behind.

The moment we try to look for signs that we are in the wrong place, we
will begin to misalign, misinterpret, and misplace. We will start to see challenges as obstacles and assume that means "Hey, wrong way!" We will
foresee need in the future and assume that means "Find this right now!"
We will see others passing by, label them as competition, and assume that
means "You should be further along!"

Until we remember—JESUS. It is the game changer for how we run today.
Refocusing on His character allows us to press reset, wherever we are at in
the race, and start again. As He infuses our minds with peace, becomes our
IV of energy to sustain our pace, and invigorates our souls with regained

passion, we realize the discouragement was merely introspective. It was never meant to be our forecast for the future!

His peace + His promises + His plans = a pace of grace, a permanent joy, and a place of safety.

Fear should never have control of the wheel. It forgets who we are following, gets trapped in "all the feels," and forfeits the race. Fear causes us to forget that the pressure is on the shoulders of the Most High God.

Faith always takes it back to Jesus. It gets our focus off ourselves and opens our eyes. As it remembers the heart of who we are trusting, our entire body recalibrates and we remain in the race. We are steadfast, sure-footed, and sealed in victory.

What we choose to remember decides everything about the way we run, and the way we run determines the reality we experience. If we find ourselves tired, drained, or discouraged, let's reassess our source. We have access to the Maker of heaven and earth, the ultimate Coach, and He withholds nothing from us. We can trust Him, His timing, and His plans for us.

Prayer

Hey Jesus, thank You for always being available and willing to help me reset my focus and recalibrate my thoughts. Remind me that my race is unique and specific. Keep my eyes fixed ahead and place my feet on solid ground. In Jesus' name,

AMEN.

Intimacy Requires Integrity

Before they call I will answer; while
they are yet speaking I will hear.

ISAIAH 65:24 ESV

Can you imagine how strange it would be if in one of your friendships or in your marriage you only acknowledged that relationship in private? When it was just you and that person, things were golden! But when you hit the streets and other people were watching, you acted as though you did not know them.

Now imagine if you had a relationship with someone and you only spoke to them in public. How strange would that be? Even when you had the opportunity to build a stronger relationship or actually get to know them, you stuck to the small talk and the quick interchanges that happen in public settings.

Both of these seem so strange when we think about them in terms of a friendship or a marriage. However, we often treat our relationship with Jesus in one of these ways and then wonder why we feel either ashamed or distant. The thing is—if our relationship with Jesus is sheerly in private and we are ashamed of the gospel or afraid to be bold when others are around, we are starving Him of the glory He deserves. This lack of confidence in His name keeps us from really stepping into the promises He has for us, as we become more focused on our curated perception than on experiencing His presence.

And then vice versa, when we only spend time with Jesus at church on Sundays or at Tuesday Bible study, we don't allow intimacy to build between our hearts and His. Until we make Him first and foremost, we will continue to operate out of striving and a performance-based faith. We also will never comprehend the joy, freedom, and grace found in surrendering our lives to Him! Abundance is never found through obligation but rather through devotion. When we prioritize time with Jesus on a daily basis in the confines of our own home when no one is watching, it feels natural to worship Him in a sanctuary when everyone is watching. Our actions in public are merely a continuation of our adoration in private.

Would you say that your relationship with Jesus is one of integrity in both your private and public life? We shouldn't be afraid to admit that we need help either pursuing Him privately or praising Him publicly. When we humbly ask for Him to show us how, He meets us in our need and reveals Himself more as He reminds us that He fulfills all our needs. Intimacy with the One who made us will only be possible when we get honest with our lives and allow Him to change us from the inside out.

Prayer

Hey Jesus, thank You for the way You continue to pursue me and call me back to You. Help me grow in godliness so that I can learn Your heart and reflect You in my life. You don't need me, but You love me and desire my company—thank You for that. In Jesus' name,

AMEN.

The Language of Both

They desire a better country, that is, a heavenly
one. Therefore God is not ashamed to be called
their God, for he has prepared for them a city.

HEBREWS 11:16 ESV

The language of both. The journey in-
between. The knowing of gray. The space that
is required to get to the other side.

We find ourselves here so often and wonder how we
can feel two wildly different things at the very same
moment.

How is it so? Are we doing it wrong? Did we miss something?

But the longer we travel and the more we see God, the more we understand that the path to being with Him is winding and sometimes weary
while also the greatest adventure of our lives. It is marked with immense
joy and intense suffering, and the presence of one does not diminish the
existence of the other. Rather, it is the experience of both that helps us
realize the difference.

The depths of grief reveal the heights of joy.
The paralysis of fear highlights the momentum of courage.
The numbing that comes from bitterness contrasts with the invigoration
that happens in celebration.
The strength required for battle makes us yearn for the restful posture of
peace.

In experiencing both, we see humanity. Our hearts are very much alive and our minds are active in pursuit of discovery. Our feet are doing their best to fervently walk on this earth; we know, in the very deepest place, that they were not meant for this world.

Foreigners traveling through, we are aware that perfection isn't possible and the pressure is real. But His love will see us through.

Grace. There's so much for us here. Because our Father is aware of the paradox we feel in the heart that He wove. Step by step, He reminds us to keep going.

We can be expectant about what is ahead while still feeling wary in the uncertainty. We can feel encouraged by how far we've come and also weary about how long the journey seems. We can be both joyful about what is in our hands and disappointed about what we had to let go.

The King of kings is the same One who gave His life to serve. It is the most confusing and beautiful "both" of our lives. May it refresh our hearts in the space we are in now—this space of navigating how to live on earth while being crafted for heaven.

Prayer

Hey Jesus, thank You for the reminder that life is often not "either-or" but the language of "both." You help me sort out my emotions and remain in the present while always keeping my mind fixed on heaven. Give me grace for the now and help me prepare for what's to come. In Jesus' name,

AMEN.

Our Great Hallelujah

Worthy are you, our LORD and God,
to receive glory and honor and power,
for you created all things, and by your
will they existed and were created.

REVELATION 4:11 ESV

Who is our God?
To get to know Him is to be in awe of Him.
To sit in His presence is to experience peace.
To receive His grace is being covered
by an eternal blanket of protection.
To be founded upon His truth is a sturdy place
no earthly thing can shake.
To be nestled in His arms is
to feel the warmth of tenderness.
To live by His strength is to have access
to a wealth of power nothing can beat.
Our hallelujah.
Nothing has to change for everything to shift
as we refocus our eyes on His goodness and take a deep breath.
Once again, remembering He is near.
Above the waves, amid the troubles, again and again He saves us.

When our hearts forget to sing "Hallelujah," He helps us still. He helps
us find gratitude and hope again—knowing the corners of our hearts and
whispering into every space.

We don't have to know anything more than what we already know about
God to experience unwavering peace, have courage in the unknown, and
carry forth with expectation of how His hands will move. For if we knew

all that He knows, we would pray for exactly what He gives. We would yearn for the things He is already doing. He is God. Yahweh. The Great I Am. He withholds no good thing and counts us as righteous when we believe.

He is the healer of our bodies. He is the holder of our future. He is the handcrafter of our souls. He is the helper of our present troubles. He is the handler of our deepest fears. He is the hero of all our battles. He is the hallelujah we can always exclaim.

Holy, holy, holy.
That is our God.
And how do we respond?
We rest knowing He is watching over us.
All is well with a soul led by the Shepherd.

Prayer

Hey Jesus, thank You for choosing to claim me and love me even though You don't need me. You are all-glorious, forever constant, and worthy of my entire life praising Your name. Help me honor You with my life. In Jesus' name,

AMEN.

Get Out of Your Head

We demolish arguments and every
pretension that sets itself up against the
knowledge of God, and we take captive every
thought to make it obedient to Christ.

II CORINTHIANS 10:5 NIV

One of the greatest strategies Satan uses is that
he tries to convince us there is no battle. It's no
big deal! We aren't "worth it." "Get comfortable!"
he says. He tells us to do what we want and give our
minds to whatever pleases us in the moment. He is
desperately hoping we fall prey to this lie. Because when
we do, we DO THE WORK FOR HIM. He doesn't have
to work to break through our gates because we left them open.
He simply walks in, introduces a thought, and says, "Hey, spend your
time on this. Isn't this interesting?" Or "Hey, did you see what ____ said?
Doesn't that make you angry?" Or "Are you aware how little you have in
the bank? Doesn't that freak you out?" Or "What about the road ahead?
Your bag seems pretty light; think that'll cover you?"

He just wants us restless. Restless in our minds while feeling paralyzed in
our bodies. Hoping we accept it as truth and do our best to remedy the
situation with what's in our control, producing striving, disappointment,
and ultimately defeat. But it always, always, always starts with our minds.
That's where he weaves the web and spins the snowball.

But, Jesus. He asks us gently, "Hey, where did you find that thought?" He
scoops us up and questions, "Who brought this to your attention? I told
you that is tomorrow's business." He knows who planted the thought and
how we've watered its roots out of fear and emotion. He is fully aware of

every thought we've had since. And so He reminds us: this is a WAR, not a game—an all-out, absolute, brutal quest for your attention and, ultimately, your soul.

Comfort is not an option.

Armor up. (Ephesians 6).
Recognize the enemy's attacks. (I Peter 5:8)
Replace lies with truth. (Psalm 86:11)
Speak life. (Proverbs 18:21)
Declare victory. (Colossians 1:13–14)
"And the God of peace will crush Satan under your feet shortly"
(Romans 16:20 NKJV).

The enemy is terrified of your future. Don't give him your present, and he has no chance at stealing God's destiny for your life. Get serious about the war for your mind because it's happening whether or not you fight. But never ever ever forget—we know how this ends.

You got this. How do I know? Because God's got this.

Prayer

Hey Jesus, thank You for continually reminding me of the power of my thoughts. Guard my mind in You; align my thoughts with ones that reflect Your truth and grace. You have already sealed the victory for me. In Jesus' name,

AMEN.

Everything we say
or do will either illuminate
or obscure the character
of God. Sanctification
is the process of joyfully
growing luminous.

JEN WILKIN

Seen + Significant

So that you may live a life worthy of the LORD and please Him in every way: bearing fruit in every good work, growing in the knowledge of God.

COLOSSIANS 1:10 NIV

It's really, really hard to show up and give our all and our best in a place where we feel people don't realize or recognize our worth or our value.

Don't they see what we sacrifice?
Don't they realize all that we do every day?
Don't they understand how heavy this load is?
Don't they comprehend that others around us aren't doing their share?
Do they even care?

Whether it be in our role at our workplace, in parenthood, in our relationships, at church, or just in our daily lives as we contribute to the world around us—wherever we find ourselves—we all struggle with this sometimes.

And it is so tempting to short-circuit our service or limit what we give when we feel like it's not seen or significant to those around us. As humans, we crave for others to understand that our shoulders are weighed down from the load we've been carrying. But the BEAUTY and the HARD part about being children of the King is that other people's awareness of our contribution is not needed for us to remain consistent in how we show up.

We have the ability to give our best to every space we are called to, even when it isn't recognized. How? Because we are SEEN by God. And should He choose to open their eyes, well, that would be nice. But even if not, our lives are meant to be a continual response to the grace we have **ALREADY** received, not a reaction to the gift or gratitude we hope we receive from others. And though this is so difficult when it's personal and close to home, it's also freeing. Empowering.

When our hands and our hearts cling to Jesus tighter than the affirmation or acknowledgment of anyone around us, we will experience fulfillment.

And this kind of fulfillment opens our eyes so wide to the mercy of where we are that we have no choice but to respond in gratitude.

It's okay to want to be seen. It's human. But when we can saturate our souls in the truth of being seen by our Savior, we will be powerfully effective where we are. When we feel unappreciated or undervalued, let's ask Jesus to remind us of our significance in the place that we stand. As we are reminded that He has already affirmed us, we can consistently contribute to the world around us because of His character. What a gift.

Prayer

Hey Jesus, thank You for positioning me with purpose and for affirming who I am before I ever do anything of use. When I feel undervalued by those around me, help me look to You. I desire to remain consistent and generous because of Your grace. In Jesus' name,

AMEN.

In Everything, Give Praise

Through him then let us continually offer
up a sacrifice of praise to God, that is, the
fruit of lips that acknowledge his name.

HEBREWS 13:15 ESV

If your prayer has not been answered, will you
still choose to praise?
If your blessing has not come, will you still choose
to praise?
If your pain is still present, will you still choose to
praise?
If your dream has been delayed, will you still choose to
praise?
If your story isn't what you expected, will you still choose to
praise?

It's easy to *say* we'll praise God—until we're faced with a personal need or
a deep valley. Until we desperately yearn for something and we can't seem
to focus on anything else.

When it feels like everyone else is walking in the Promised Land and we
feel like the wilderness will not end, what will we do?

We have a choice, even when it seems like we don't, to lift up the name of
Jesus and speak life in the places that feel dry, dead, discouraging, or distant.

In the midst of searching for a spouse, PRAISE.
In the midst of the cancer treatments, PRAISE.
In the midst of the financial strain, PRAISE.
In the midst of the fight with our addiction, PRAISE.

In the midst of discovering our purpose, PRAISE.
In the midst of the infertility journey, PRAISE.
In the midst of searching for deeper friendships, PRAISE.

I know it is so light to say because so much of this is heavy, but praise is not a celebratory reaction to things going our way. It is a decision—it's our WEAPON—to gaining supernatural vision, even in the bleakest of circumstances.

Praise is the proactive approach to our prayers, knowing that the One who made our hearts is already fully aware of everything we need. He withholds nothing good from those who love Him. And EVEN IF our circumstances remain, the pain comes back, the heartache continues, or the wait seems to never end, praise can remain on our lips.

Because what if the KEY to our joy and our strength and our patience and our hope is not the outward change of our experience but the peace that invaded our lives through our praise? What if we focus on seeing God for all that He ALREADY is no matter what life seems to give us? Even if nothing changes around us, He is transforming the heart within us. What a gift.

Prayer

Hey Jesus, thank You for reminding me that You are always working, always in control, and always good. When I feel discouraged or defeated, help me speak life. Give me supernatural vision to see life through Your eyes and keep praise on my lips. In Jesus' name,

AMEN.

Feels Like Winter

He said to them, "It is not for you to know times or seasons that the Father has fixed by his own authority."

ACTS 1:7 ESV

Here. This place. The one that you are hoping passes in the night or decides to skip you in line—this place. The one that removes your previous distractions or misplaced priorities and makes you feel a bit . . . naked.

Exposed to yourself in a way that you must evaluate, knowing that you cannot simply replace what has been removed in order to experience refreshment. This place that has stripped away so much of what made you comfortable, and you feel as though you can no longer offer shade to those around you. Do you know this place?

These difficult seasons, or "winters" as we call them, are required. We all would like to do without them, and yet we are fully aware that it is through the winters we have already endured that we gained the fortitude to keep going, the friendships to encourage us, and the faith to ground us. Winter takes away what we thought made us valuable and reminds us that the Creator never needed our leaves for the shade, our fruit for the food, or our stature to find strength. In these seasons where we feel a bit exposed, His nearness is overwhelming.

Winter invites the covering and solidifies the intimacy so that when springtime arrives, our gratitude and praise are the only worthy responses.

This place—whatever brought us here or however it looks—doesn't have to be outwardly tragic to feel inwardly tough. It can just be a time when we aren't sure: we aren't sure of what's next, we aren't sure of what's around us, or we aren't sure of much at all.

But HERE we become very sure of God. We are reminded that seasons are required for all good things to remain alive. We are still growing here, still blooming. It's precisely in this place that we gain grit, deepen our empathy, and strengthen our roots. Flourishing always requires the stripping away so that the new can come.

So while we wait, as we trek through the rough terrain of winter, may we hold joy very close.

Knowing that here, we are blooming.
Knowing that here, fresh grace is making good ground.
Knowing that here, Jesus is the only covering we need.

Winter reminds us that we never needed the adornment of leaves to be adored by the Creator. So as we wait, we can walk expectantly. We can still hold joy while waiting for spring.

Prayer

Hey Jesus, thank You for being consistent and dependable, even when everything else in my life feels fickle and unsure. Plant Your truth in my heart and remind me that no season lasts forever. You are always doing something new. In Jesus' name,

AMEN.

Up to the Mountain

Indeed, I count everything as loss because of the surpassing worth of knowing Christ Jesus my LORD. For his sake I have suffered the loss of all things and count them as rubbish, in order that I may gain Christ.

PHILIPPIANS 3:8 ESV

Gathering with others is fun, isn't it? It provides entertainment, brings happy noise, and makes traditions much more exciting to celebrate. However, think about the romantic relationships in your life—whether someone you dated in the past, your spouse now, or the one you hope to have. Ask yourself: If your time spent with them was mainly facilitated through events, gatherings, and community-driven happenings, how well would you really get to know them? How intimate would that relationship feel?

Community is crucial. Praying together is powerful. Going to church is nourishment for our bodies and our souls. However, there is never a replacement for our time alone with God. When we take the time to be still with our Savior and give our time and our energy to just being with Him, He recenters us and refreshes our soul.

Jesus, the only perfect person and the actual Son of God, performed miracle after miracle on earth. One of His most talked-about miracles is when He fed the five thousand people with only five loaves of bread and two fish. We usually don't look to see what happened after this miracle, though, do we? What does one do after taking part in such an incredible expression of God's faithfulness?

Matthew 14:23 tells us that after Jesus sent the crowd away and the disciples left on a boat, He "went up on a mountainside by Himself to pray"

(NIV). He wanted to talk to His Father. He never let His pride puff Him up after a miracle was performed; He knew that His communication with His Father was His lifeline. Jesus deeply valued His followers while on this earth, and He invested greatly in His disciples, teaching them with His words and actions. When I read the Bible, it stands out to me that if Jesus were physically here now, He would prioritize His solitude with His Father far more than He would look forward to any potluck dinner, podcast episode, or prayer rally.

We can be really good at picking songs to sing, catering events, and buying all the Bible study books imaginable, but until we get real, honest, and alone before God, we will always feel depleted in our community. Getting together with others is such an important part of our walk with Jesus, but if we don't know the Jesus we get together to talk about and worship, what is the point? Without disciplining ourselves to have alone time with God, our lives begin to look a lot like performance. However, when we follow the example Jesus set for us, we become restored in His presence and we have the ability to take part in miracles!

Wherever we are and whatever we do, we must never think we are too important or too busy "to go up to the mountainside" and be with our heavenly Father.

Prayer

Hey Jesus, thank You for desiring to spend time with me and for crafting my soul to yearn for time alone with You. Help me not get distracted, but let my time with You be a source of nourishment, and let my fulfillment be found in You. Quiet my soul and open my eyes. In Jesus' name,

AMEN.

God-Dreaming

Faithful is He who calls you, and
He also will bring it to pass.

I THESSALONIANS 5:24 NASB

It has always been perplexing to me how we can use the same term for extremely different concepts. We say that we had a terrible "dream" last night, referencing the nightmare we wouldn't want to revisit or the crazy journey we went on for five hours in our sleep, but we can only recollect a fragment of the experience. We then use this same term to reference the intense desires we have for our life's work.

"What is your dream?" We ask ourselves and others this question, not even quite sure what we are actually asking. We are hoping to find the answer that will help us fulfill the desire of our lives: We want to leave behind something that matters. Whether it be through the avenue of a full-time vocation, a part-time hobby, or in the service of motherhood or fatherhood itself, we want to feel as though all our doing is amounting to something greater than ourselves and bigger than today.

Scripture tells us that the goal of our lives is getting to know Jesus and, in turn, making sure others do too. This can be done a thousand different ways, but the purpose is still the same: to understand the heart of the One who is in control so that we can spend our lives in total surrender. It is only through intimacy with our heavenly Father that we release our trust to Him. And as we hand Him our trust, He hands us joy, peace, hope, kindness, patience, self-control, and love. He graces us with the wisdom, gifts, and resources to make an impact through the works of our human hands.

Sometimes we feel like the dream within our hearts does match that elusive dream we have when we sleep. Both feel far-fetched, uncertain, and confusing. We don't know how to run quick enough or rest well enough to hold either one closely, but the truth is, if something is a God-dream meant to radiate His love to a watching world, He will not let it become a fleeting thought. As we pursue His heart, pray about what He is asking of us, and push out of our comfort zones, He will lead us.

God-dreams will never ask us to run at a pace that is unhealthy, compromise our future for the sake of someone else's present, or push us away from His voice. If it scares us because it forces our reliance on only Jesus, that is often a good sign. We can trust that if great faith is required, great faithfulness will meet us there. But we are never the ones who give it credence or purpose; it is Him.

How do we live out a God-dream? We hang out with God. It's His dream after all.

Prayer

Hey Jesus, thank You for the dreams You have placed inside of me—God-dreams that are holy, important, and valuable. Help me search after You, and give me the courage and insight to know what to do and how to live. I want to glorify You. In Jesus' name,

AMEN.

Unseen Battles

To speak evil of no one, to avoid
quarreling, to be gentle, and to show
perfect courtesy toward all people.

TITUS 3:2 ESV

What if we assumed when interacting with others that everyone is fighting an unseen battle—a battle the world knows little about? Assumptions can be dangerous, but I think this one may be an exception.

The truth is, we know so little of what others are walking through, even when we think we know. Because often, they don't even realize the weight of the hardship, the strain of the relationship, or the way they've had to adapt and cope. They don't see their own fragility, so how could we see it? And so even if they would tell us, they are discovering the battle themselves and unaware they've even been at war.

What about the strangers we pass during the day or the casual acquaintance we see at the grocery store? Our interactions are so limited, and yet we make judgments or assumptions with only the itty-bitty amount of information that we are given on the surface. Usually, we both are unaware of what is really going on in one another's lives, and our information is skewed. Many times, our countenance or theirs is curated by what we are hoping to mask or the battle we are currently fighting.

And in the midst of our overwhelming circumstances, our stress, our busyness, and even our delight and celebration, we tend to forget this. Because if we chose to remember the unseen battles, we would have to offer undeserved grace, unusual kindness, and uncomfortable gentleness. It would ask something of us we don't always want to give.

But when we are the receiver of it? Oh, it alters our lives. When we are the ones fighting the battle and someone covers us with lavish mercy or forgives the hard stuff, we see Jesus.

What if your own progress isn't on the other side of your perfection but in the hands of the healing you allow yourself to receive? To realize we are fighting battles that we often don't publicize or even perceive is to give ourselves a blanket in the midst of our cold day.

All of us would experience richer relationships and more encounters that affected eternity if we constantly asked the Lord, "Will You help me see them/me as You do?"

What if the victory for someone else's unseen battle could be achieved through the gentleness, kindness, or forgiveness we offered them without even knowing what they were fighting? Well, that would look like Jesus.

Prayer

Hey Jesus, thank You for the reminder that we all are fighting battles that aren't obvious on the surface. Humble our hearts and help us see ourselves and others through Your eyes. Grace us with the gentleness, kindness, and forgiveness we need to look more like You. In Jesus' name,

AMEN.

Smells like Smoke

Do not be conformed to this world, but be transformed by the renewal of your mind, that by testing you may discern what is the will of God, what is good and acceptable and perfect.

ROMANS 12:2 ESV

Have you walked through the airport and seen the smoking rooms that are scattered throughout the terminals? If you get near the door, the smoke is overwhelming once it opens. Lots of people with lots of smoke means that one will naturally smell like smoke when leaving.

Now imagine that a nonsmoker says, "Since I am a nonsmoker, it won't affect me." This would seem laughable because despite our best attempts to dodge the smell, it would be nearly impossible to leave without absorbing the smell of smoke. And yet, this is often what we do in our own lives with so many things!

We place ourselves in situations that aren't beneficial or around people that are toxic to our health, and we claim that it won't affect us. We surround ourselves with riches, resources, or relationships that do not align with our hopeful destination and then act surprised when our lives are not fulfilling our souls.

However, the truth is that our thoughts, words, and actions are always affected by the places and people we surround ourselves with, even when we don't realize it. Whether or not our intention was to leave smelling like smoke, we will begin to reflect the decisions we make, the places we frequent, and the relationships we hold close.

How do we radiate Jesus? We position ourselves in places that value His Word. We prioritize relationships by treasuring Him in our conversations. We pursue healthy habits and rhythms that help us abide in Jesus, not distract us from Him.

The hard part about this truth is realizing that sometimes we are the smoke to others and that our current lifestyle, in whatever capacity, does not leave a positive impact on ourselves or others. No matter how much we try to control or temper it, we will naturally deposit into others what is being deposited into us. So, what are we filling ourselves with and therefore allowing to spill out?

Looking like Jesus does not mean always smelling like roses or having a picturesque view of reality; however, it does require us to keep truth at the forefront of our minds and remember that we are part of God's kingdom and represent Him to the world. Let's remember that God's instruction always leads to peace and that His boundary lines, even when we don't understand them, are drawn in pleasant places.

Prayer

Hey Jesus, thank You for equipping me with the boldness and authority to resist temptation and choose the path of life in my choices and relationships. Help me prioritize eternity and give me discernment with my words and actions. Keep me in step with You. In Jesus' name,

AMEN.

In Awe

Let all the earth fear the LORD; let all the inhabitants of the world stand in awe of Him.

PSALM 33:8 NASB

When you think of a picturesque setting, what comes to your mind? Imagine that. Think about the snow that falls on the mountaintops in Colorado, the crystal-clear waters that greet the white sandy beaches in Mexico, or the unbelievable layers of rock that are on display in the Grand Canyon.

Imagining these places or seeing pictures, our mouths drop open and our eyes get big. Even when we are getting a front-row seat to the beauty in front of us, the majestic nature of its makeup seems like too much to bear. We are in awe—we realize our smallness, we grapple with our lack of control, we witness the beauty of creation in its most raw forms—and our hearts fight with our heads to comprehend our view.

How is it that we can see these sights, experience these trips, and get a view of "heaven on earth" and so quickly forget it a week later? Our sense of awe is then quickly covered up by our to-do lists and our current reality. We feel so bogged down by the view outside our own window or in the mirror we face that the awe we felt before feels so far away.

We were created to be in awe. This phrasing, often used nonchalantly, is how we would remain if we truly knew and believed in the Lord's goodness. Being in awe is a quality of childlike faith, when we become so enamored with the One caring for us that we stop worrying about what will happen next, how it will happen, or if we are where we hoped we would be. Because how could we not just sit and want to be with someone so gentle, so kind, so forgiving, so generous, so perfect?

He does not offer us the gifts of nature and beauty so that we become obsessed with the place; He lets us experience these tangible forms of grace so that we become consumed with the Creator Himself. Because if the works of His hands are that mighty and beautiful, how much more must His presence be?

May we sit with Him, talk with Him, learn from Him, and just desire to be with Him. May we be in awe, knowing that being a student of the King of kings is the greatest calling we could have in this life.

Prayer

Dear Jesus, thank You for being who You are—Your power and Your beauty are too great to describe. Help us be students and seekers of Your presence, realizing that our greatest gift is always the Creator of the creation. In Jesus' name,

AMEN.

Our True Identity

And the LORD said to Moses, "This very thing
that you have spoken I will do, for you have found
favor in my sight, and I know you by name."

EXODUS 33:17 ESV

Cleere is an unusual name. It's a family name
that was passed down from my great-grandfather,
and I have gone by "Claire" more times than I
can count, most people thinking it's my accent.
Don't get me wrong; I am not sure anything else even
fits me, and I love my name, but it definitely ensures I
will never find it written on a magnet at Cracker Barrel.

Because it's uncommon, I sometimes will use my last name or
another name when I go to Panera, Starbucks, or somewhere that
requires someone to say my name out loud. On one particular day, I was
eating lunch with a friend and chose to go by "Sophie." I know, don't ask.
Twenty minutes into our conversation, I realized I still didn't have my food
and went to inquire about where it might be. Turns out, they had in fact
called for "Sophie" all throughout the restaurant and she was nowhere to
be found. Whoops. Try explaining that one to the cashier!

I mention this story because I think we sometimes redefine what God has
already named and then wonder why we feel forgotten. We are waiting on
a permission slip to receive the blessing that God has already placed on
our lives, but we must walk in our true identity before that can take place.
We don't need a new name or a more impressive résumé; we need the
stamped declaration of a fulfilled life that our Creator has already placed
within our grasp.

Sometimes we feel like because we have been identifying with characteristics that do not align with our God-given identity, we owe something to that false identity or to the people we have convinced of our false identity. However, we don't have to justify, defend, or rationalize what was; we can simply accept the gift of where we are going and who is holding us and focus on who we are in Jesus.

What might be keeping you from sitting at the Father's table right now? Are you trying to earn what can only be gifted through grace? Have you forgotten your God-given identity and replaced it with the world's idea of beauty and belonging? Your name has been called and your inheritance is already secure. Dig into what your heavenly Father says about you and write it over your life.

We don't need to wonder if we've been called; He has named us, spoken life over us, and positioned us for promise. Only our Creator gets the honor of determining who we are and who He intends us to be.

Prayer

Hey Jesus, thank You for calling us by name and for establishing our identity. Show us how to walk firmly and boldly in our God-given identity, trusting that Your say is final and true. In Jesus' name,

AMEN.

Stained for Significance

Arise, shine, for your light has come, and
the glory of the LORD has risen upon you.

ISAIAH 60:1 ESV

Have you ever taken a moment to really study
a stained glass window? Its intricacies and
the work it takes are obvious from a simple
observation.

The cool thing about a stained glass window is
that before anything is ever created, there is a design
crafted. This design is detailed and thoughtfully planned
out, taking into account every millimeter of space used.
Every window tells a story, so that even though the design is two-
dimensional, when the light fills the creation, the story comes alive. The
colors chosen were not by coincidence; each one plays a part in a much
larger role. The brilliance of the window requires the light for its impact;
otherwise, it becomes just an impressive, complex design with unlimited
but untapped potential.

As you reflect on these masterful pieces of art, you can't help but notice
that we are so similar in nature. Before anyone else was aware of even the
thought of us, He had a plan in motion. As He wove us together, speaking life into our bones, gifting us with unique and important qualities, and
positioning us exactly where we needed to be, He created us and said, "It
is really good." His masterpiece.

The role of the glass, our role, is not to be magnificent in and of itself; it is
simply supposed to BE, soaking in the light and reflecting the light's rays
through its perfectly imperfect creation. We do not have to add to ourselves

what He has not already given us. Simply by being transparent and showing up as ourselves, we allow the light of Jesus to pass through and we get to experience the radiance that comes from walking in our calling. The design and purpose of our lives was constructed by our Creator; this means that the pressure is off our shoulders to make something of ourselves that is sufficient or significant on this earth. It is only by responding to the covering of grace and love of Jesus that we access the fulfillment and purpose that we crave.

Are we letting the light in? Are we working really hard to earn our space, explain ourselves, or impress the watching world, not realizing that His handiwork is only made complete by resting in Him? We did not get a say in how we were designed because we are not God; we must trust that whatever He has given us, wherever He has placed us, whomever He has surrounded us with, and whatever our lives look like, He uses every piece of our story for His glory. Our job is simply to be in His presence, and the rest will come.

Prayer

Hey Jesus, thank You for the uniqueness, purpose, and significance You have placed on my life. You are the Creator of the world and of my heart. I rest in this truth and the peace that comes with it. Help me be transparent and receive Your light so that others see You in me. In Jesus' name,

AMEN.

Identity
apart from
God is
inherently
unstable.

TIMOTHY KELLER

Will You Let It Go?

Jesus told him, "If you want to be perfect,
go and sell all your possessions and give
the money to the poor, and you will have
treasure in heaven. Then come, follow Me."

MATTHEW 19:21 NLT

The story of the rich young ruler is found in three of the Gospels: Matthew, Mark, and Luke. It is about a man who had great wealth and asked Jesus, "Teacher, what good deed must I do to have eternal life?" (Matthew 19:16 NLT). Jesus responds to this man by quoting several commandments, all of which the man says he follows. So Jesus then tells him that if he truly wants to seek righteousness, he should sell all his possessions and give to the poor.

Because Jesus knows everything, He already knew the man was adhering to the commandments that were comfortable for him. However, Jesus knew that there was one thing he was holding on to tighter than he was clinging to Jesus, and that was his wealth.

Jesus asked him to sacrifice the one thing that was keeping him hostage so that he could experience the freedom Jesus wanted to give him. But his fear, pride, and desire for comfort kept him enslaved. Jesus already knew what the man could not see—that despite the rich young ruler's following of certain instruction, he still did not fully trust God. His tight grip on his possessions had less to do with money and more to do with his desire for security.

What is it for us? We all have things that we know God has asked us to let go of so that we can walk in the joy and hope He offers. Do we trust Him with some parts of our lives but limit our obedience to the places we feel comfortable letting go?

Until we are willing to truly surrender it all to Him, we will continue to work from a place of striving, operate from a place of self-protection, and live from a place of fear. Fulfillment is not found in attaining everything we thought we wanted; it is discovered when we realize He is actually all we need. Jesus does not want us to live from a rigid set of rules—as the rich young ruler did—crossing off our obligations and thinking that is His idea of a true follower; He wants us to trust Him enough to run wholeheartedly after Him.

God has greater things in store for us—all of us. May we desire the fruit of righteousness way more than anything this world could give. Nothing we are ever asked to give up can compare to the grace we receive in return.

Prayer

Hey Jesus, thank You for never letting us settle for a comfortable life; You desire for us to taste the fullness You offer. Help us surrender anything that keeps us from wholeheartedly serving You, even if that thing seems good. You are worthy of it all. In Jesus' name,

AMEN.

Hand in Hand into the Deep

We urge you, brothers and sisters, warn those who are idle and disruptive, encourage the disheartened, help the weak, be patient with everyone.

I THESSALONIANS 5:14 NIV

Everyone on the beach was enamored by it—the sea turtle nest was full of hatchlings that were almost ready to make their exit and head for the ocean. There were people designated to keep watch over the nests and make sure that nothing disturbed the survival process for these baby turtles. I had seen nests before, but my interest was piqued as I thought about this animal and its journey to the ocean. As I researched, I was reminded that these baby turtles always make their exit from the nest in unison, resembling a pot of boiling water as they spill into the sea. They all travel together as this increases their chance of escaping from predators like sea birds, wild dogs, foxes, and raccoons. Traveling together also lessens the risk that they will slow their pace and die of dehydration from the intensity of the sun.

Isn't this relatively true for us as humans? While the threat may not seem as apparent or violent, there is very much an enemy that wants to isolate us, scare us, and rob us of a full life. He knows that if he can get us alone and focused on the wrong things, we will forget our purpose or give in to the temptations that surround us. Instead of the beach sun dehydrating us, it will be the pressure from the world that drains our energy and makes us thirst for things that never satisfy.

Running this race of life with others was never intended to be about comparing our journey to others' journeys; rather, it is about being in community with like-minded believers who spur us on, remind us of our purpose, and allow us to travel into deep waters. This "turtle pace," as we will call it, is a family effort toward accessing the wondrous life that God has planned for us.

If you feel like you are struggling with feeling lonely, finding solid friendships, or understanding what a real community looks like, why do you think that is? Are you afraid you aren't good enough? Does the need for intimacy scare you? Does the proximity of others in your personal space unnerve you? Do you feel like you have to practice self-preservation, looking after yourself rather than the needs of others, to ensure you are protected?

The goal of baby turtles is that as many turtles as possible will make it to the deep, blue waters and experience the very life they were created to live. This is the goal for the human race, too, but until we position ourselves around others who are mission-minded, brave, and focused on the ultimate goal of sharing God's love with the world, we will miss living life to its fullest capacity.

Prayer

Hey Jesus, thank You for designing me to live in community with those around me, filling me with courage, strength, and hope. Help me remain accountable, vulnerable, and helpful to my brothers and sisters. Help me know when it's time to huddle up and when it's time to step out of my comfort zone. In Jesus' name,

AMEN.

The Good Shepherd

I am the good shepherd. The good shepherd lays down his life for the sheep.

JOHN 10:11 ESV

The path was unpredictable and full of random turns. We had only a limited view in front of us, and what we could see felt daunting. It was hot and muggy, and I felt myself getting more tired as my discouragement grew. How were we going to get to our destination? I knew that this was not the first time this tour guide had led a group through a rough patch; he had already told our group that this was his eighth year serving as a tour guide, and his veteran status ensured our safety.

Because my exhaustion felt imminent, I kept thinking, "But what if I miss a turn and don't realize it? What if I can't keep up and he doesn't see that I'm far behind?" I continued to pick up my feet and pressed onward, hoping that my soul would settle down. Fear was not an emotion I often experienced, but it felt loud and in charge on this particular day. I had chosen to go the "advanced route" on this hike and was quickly regretting that decision.

When we finally took our rest break, I knew I needed to recalibrate my mind. As I turned my focus back to Jesus, it almost felt like a literal earth shift happened, and yet I knew nothing was actually happening in real time. However, I realized that my fear was stemming from placing my confidence in my ability to follow instead of the guide's ability to lead. My distorted view of reality was shaped by my irrational fear of being left behind based on my own inability to keep up.

But Jesus. Isn't it always "But Jesus"? He was reminding my heart that He is the Great Shepherd. He is the One who pursues the lost sheep. Just like in my relationship with Him, my confidence to get to the other side can never be based on my keen ability to follow or my own endurance; rather, it is founded in my trust of who is leading me.

Do I believe that Jesus cares more for me than for our desired destination? Is the hope of His heart really to help me know Him? If so, then my fear of being left behind, forgotten, or incapable is no longer on the table. I am His sheep, and He has already proven that He will lay down His life for mine. His priority is my heart, His joy is my adoration, and His mission is that I would remain in step with Him. Therefore, I do not need to be afraid.

That hike turned out to be one of my favorite experiences to date. What I learned on that hike can be applied to my faith journey. When I recenter my heart and remember my role, my fears disappear. As long as I follow my Leader, my passage and victory have already been solidified. He just asks that I take one step at a time.

Prayer

Hey Jesus, thank You for being my Good Shepherd—for leading me down paths of righteousness, through the wilderness, and into the depths of Your promises. Help me believe that Your priority is my heart. May I never leave Your sight. Help me focus on that goodness. In Jesus' name,

AMEN.

Overjoyed at His success

He has come from above and is greater than
anyone else. We are of the earth, and we speak
of earthly things, but He has come from
heaven and is greater than anyone else.

JOHN 3:31 NLT

Do you remember the story of John baptizing
people in the Jordan River? Imagine John the
Baptist on one side of the river, and then imagine
Jesus on the other side. Well, John's disciples are worried because everyone is now going to the other side
of the river to get baptized by Jesus. They see the crowd
flocking to Jesus and feel frustrated by the change of pace.
When they voice this concern, John immediately reminds them
that the only reason John has this gift to baptize others is because God
gave it to him to prepare the way for the Messiah, the very One standing
on the other side of the river. The only purpose of John's existence is to
prepare the way for Jesus Himself as He makes His presence known to His
people. What the disciples are worried about becomes the very reason for
John's joy: Jesus is here, and He is stealing the show!

How often do we worry about receiving the credit for our good works?
We exhaust ourselves to complete tasks, show up well, and make good use
of our gifts and abilities. However, if the goal of our efforts is to attain a
certain perception from the watching world, then we are missing the point.
John reminds us that in order for us to reflect the heart of the Father, we
must make Jesus greater and we must make ourselves less (John 3:30). This
assertion of humility does not mean dwindled confidence, shy ambitions,
or weariness to be bold in what we do or how we do it; it is merely to
remind us that the why behind what we are doing is most important. We

are preparing the way for Jesus to return to gather His people so we can live with Him forever. If anything we do puts more stock in our earthly kingdom than His heavenly one, our red flags need to be waving.

God wants us to radiate joy, hope, and strength. He longs for us to flourish in our gifts. But the only way that we can do this and not be distracted or enamored by our own glory is to give all the glory to Him, knowing that our purpose is always to bring heaven to earth. The advancement of Jesus, whatever it requires of us, is the greatest joy we will know. The more we let Jesus "steal the show" (as if He needs our help), the more His light shines through us.

Prayer

Hey Jesus, thank You for the way that You allow me to take part in Your miracles as You bring heaven to earth. Arrest my heart and help me surrender my pride when I try to make much of myself. My purpose is building Your kingdom. In Jesus' name,

AMEN.

Our Mess, His Miracle

What we suffer now is nothing compared to the glory He will reveal to us later.

ROMANS 8:18 NLT

She had no idea that my eyes were on her life.

Life had not been kind to her lately. Amid a job transition, financial strain, discovering that her husband had had an affair, and her own insecurities, she felt like at any point another shoe would drop. However, as I watched her come to work, kindly deal with others, give her best to every task, and still speak life to others, I was amazed at what God was doing in her and through her. We had been coworkers for over a year, and her steadiness was such an example to me.

Upon telling her this one day, she responded with these exact words: "Wow, that is shocking. All this time, I had no idea that my mess was actually what revealed my strength, not removed it. Everything has felt so heavy; I can't believe you've seen light in me."

But isn't this how God works? When life presses in, He helps us persevere. When our circumstances feel hopeless, He draws us back to His well and restores us. When relationships disappoint us, He whispers into the deep chambers of our soul that we are seen, loved, and worthy of belonging. Through those moments when what is surrounding us feels like too much, He provides the grace we need for right where we are. My friend radiated the strength of Jesus, even when she felt like she could barely keep moving. Her diligence and consistency in her workplace did not make sense from an earthly perspective: How was she able to keep showing up when life wasn't showing up for her? Jesus was using the mess around her to reveal the radiance within her, and everyone around her was better for it.

Who might be watching you? What do your current struggles or circumstances allow you to reflect? It is usually in the unexpected times that others' eyes are on our lives, watching to see if the faith we sing about on the mountaintop is the same faith we cling to in the valley. Our mess can still radiate Jesus; in fact, it is the perfect breeding ground to reflect the heart of a miracle-working Father.

Prayer

Hey Jesus, thank You for seeing us in the midst of our struggles and for using everything for Your glory. Give us perspective—help us to lean in and dig deep when things seem dim, trusting that the light You are producing within us is always greater. In Jesus' name,

AMEN.

What We Can't Fix

**Blessed are the peacemakers, for
they shall be called sons of God.**

MATTHEW 5:9 ESV

I opened up my phone and read the text and
my heart sank. I could feel my stomach tie up
in knots, and my mind became consumed with
the situation all over again. How had we even
gotten to this place? With one misunderstanding
after another, it felt like we had become distant, and
neither of us was quite sure of the reason. There were
obviously some things that needed to be healed, some conversations that had to happen, and some vulnerability that
was going to have to take place. As I prayed about how to approach
it and what to say, and asked for heaven's perspective, I was waiting on
God to solidify my words and release me to go patch everything up.

Much to my surprise and dismay, I realized that God wasn't asking me to
go "fix" anything. I had tried to make everything better and kept coming
back to this place of helplessness, knowing that God was wanting me to
truly trust Him with what was beyond my control. I assume I am a person
of patience until it comes to relational discord, and then I quickly realize
that my patience is limited. Even though desiring peace is a good thing, I
had let the desire to restore this relationship become an idol. Reflecting on
my current situation and past relationships, it was obvious that any time
there was a hiccup with someone, I became consumed with fixing it. This
time, God just wanted it to be Him and me, hand in hand. I needed to
learn that maybe the larger issue wasn't the relational discord but the lack
of trust I had in Jesus to handle whatever it may be.

Unfortunately, there are some relationships and circumstances in life that we just have to let go of and leave at the cross. Our surrender does not confirm our apathy; rather, it reveals our sincere care. Because if there is any place where we'll find healing for the hard stuff and hear how to continue moving when it feels too heavy, it's at Jesus' feet. He wants us to be so confident in our relationship with Him that no matter what else is going on, we choose to keep going, look for His fingerprints, and trust Him with whatever comes.

Whether it's a relationship you're trying to white-knuckle, a situation that you desperately want to fix, or a circumstance that is consuming your attention, choose to release it into the care of your heavenly Father. Sometimes the delay is what brings illumination so reconciliation can happen. And sometimes we are just forced to dig deeper, and this delay brings us greater understanding of who our Father is.

God is powerful and good. He can fix anything that needs fixing whenever He wants to fix it. In the meantime, let's focus our attention on Him, knowing that the particulars are His specialty and His peace still covers us until the fixing gets done.

Prayer

Hey Jesus, thank You for the constant reminder that You are King over everything. Restoration, reconciliation, and redemption are Your specialty. Help us trust You with the details, knowing that what we can't fix is safely in Your loving and life-giving hands. In Jesus' name,

AMEN.

Fourth Quarter Surprises

Be strong, and let your heart take courage,
all you who wait for the LORD!

PSALM 31:24 ESV

Everyone had deemed it a loss. The stands started to empty out, and people began gathering their things. The football game wasn't over, but based on the scoreboard, it sure felt like a big *L* was going in the books. However, because I was waiting for a ride, there I sat thinking I was going to be the only fan left, other than the families of the players.

So I got comfortable and pulled my phone out. As I started to type away at an email, the crowd started hollering as we finally graced the end zone for the first time since the first quarter. The next twenty minutes proved to be one of the most exciting and resilient games of football I've ever witnessed. What we thought was going to be a shutout turned into a show-out, and our team actually ended up winning the game. As I stood up to high-five the man next to me, he said, "And that, ladies and gentlemen, is why you never give up before it's over!"

Profound. So simple and yet so true. How often do we give up on others, ourselves, or just general situations in our lives because the odds are stacked against us? Sometimes it feels silly to be the only one still in the stands, cheering anytime progress is made. This hard truth can look like sticking with a marriage that seems doomed from the outside, continuing to give of our resources in a time of scarcity, believing for healing in a medical situation that feels bleak, or standing our ground in our own lives when we have no idea how the dots will connect.

It's easy to never give up when life is favorable, but it is in the moments when it's not that we have the opportunity to develop perseverance, walk in true hope, and build our resilience. Don't you think Jesus would be so proud of His children for staying the course no matter the results? Because to be honest, I am not sure He cares much about the scoreboard; I believe as our Maker watches us clap our hands, continue walking, and choose faith, He smiles and says, "I call that a win."

Don't give up. Don't let those watching determine what you believe is possible. Stand in truth, be a trooper for others, and fight as a warrior for your own life. Because we follow the King of kings, we can remain hopeful even in the most hopeless of situations. Radiating resilience will always reveal the root of our beliefs. And our God never, ever gives up. Fourth quarter surprises are His specialty.

Prayer

Hey Jesus, thank You for providing us with opportunities to remain and operate in Your resilience; we see our faith is built here. You never give up on us, no matter how hopeless we may feel. Help us be people who believe and stay when it's easier to get discouraged and go. In Jesus' name,

AMEN.

Boiling Over

Do not be slothful in zeal, be fervent
in spirit, serve the LORD.

ROMANS 12:11 ESV

Have you ever been around someone who was
just oozing with excitement about Jesus? It was
not that they necessarily were loud about it, but
it came from a deep place in their soul that they
just really, really loved Jesus. No matter where they
were, who they were talking to, or what was happening in their life, they consistently just said, "God
is so good!"

That kind of fervency for the Lord is inspiring and challenging
as it makes those who witness it ask, "Do I live with this same kind of
enthusiasm about Jesus?"

The word *fervent* comes from the Latin word *fervens*, which means "boiling."
This matches what this word means in the original Greek, *zeontes*, "boiling in spirit." When we are fervently pursuing God, our spirit naturally
bubbles over onto ourselves and everyone we are around. As we lean in
and experience His grace, it becomes impossible not to share such revelation and hope with others.

If we find ourselves feeling stagnant or lacking the desire to spend time
with Jesus, it is not because Jesus is any less exciting; it is that we are far
too comfortable. Many times we will continue on with religious practice
and language but are not applying our faith, praying with belief that
He is listening, or stepping out in bravery. How will the faithfulness of
God overwhelm us if we aren't taking any leaps of faith? Why would we

expect to be enthusiastic about a relationship that we have simply added to our checklist?

Fervency of spirit is not an innocent excitement based on surface emotions; it is a continual decision to remember God.

Think about it—when we choose to remember God in conversations and we bring Him up, we open the door to hear stories from others about His kindness and strength. When we decide to do the hard thing, we witness His courage through us. When we show up to serve others in His name, our own souls are encouraged by the body doing what it is called to do.

And when the darkness feels imminent or things aren't okay in our lives? The fervency of our prayers helps us recall in the dark what we remembered in the light. We become beneficiaries of our own boiling over.

Being zealous for the Lord is living in awareness of just how good His grace actually is—it's awareness that we, in all moments, are continually being saved from ourselves.

Prayer

Hey Jesus, thank You for being an exciting, innovative, faithful, fresh, and enthusiastic Savior! Help me to develop a fervency for Your Word and Your presence; I want to abide in You so that I may boil over with grace and love, reflecting You in me. In Jesus' name,

AMEN.

Content with Mud Pies

When Paul said he had learned what it meant to
be content, what did he mean? Did he mean that
he had received everything he wanted?

Many times as Christians, we are told that our desires
are the issue, right? Because of our sin nature, we crave
what isn't good for us and pursue what will hurt us. And
while it is partially true, I think we hear this and immediately
assume we should forgo human desire altogether. If we can just
stop wanting anything, then we can become holy, yes?

However, it is impossible to remove desire from our being; it is what makes
us alive! The desire to choose one way or another is what makes us human
instead of robotic; it is the ability to pursue our desires that allows us to
experience love, peace, and contentment. The issue is not that our desires
are too strong or unattainable; the issue is that we usually settle for way less
than the Father intends for our lives.

C. S. Lewis said it brilliantly: "It would seem that Our Lord finds our
desires not too strong, but too weak. We are halfhearted creatures, fooling
about with drink and sex and ambition when infinite joy is offered us, like
an ignorant child who wants to go on making mud pies in a slum because
he cannot imagine what is meant by the offer of a holiday at the sea. We
are far too easily pleased.*

It seems harsh to say, but it is true: The treasures of God turn the world's idea of treasure into a mud pie. Maybe instead of wishing our desire away, we can pray for that desire to be increased from what is easy to reach for and replaced with what can never be reached. As we desire perfection in Jesus, we begin to stumble upon the beauty of being refined in His image, experiencing His gentleness as we sit with Him and learning that our half-hearted attempts to impress Him could never match our wholehearted devotion to just being around Him.

Our contentment happens as we come face-to-face with who God really is. Maybe that's what Paul meant when he said that he learned to be content in whatever circumstances life brought him; the satisfaction of his soul rested in the unchanging steadiness of God. Whether in the prison or the palace, Paul decided that his current suffering did not change his contentment because everything endured here is worth even a glimmer of heaven's gain.

Isn't it a relief to know we can always be content by desiring heaven? May we not be so easily pleased with what we can see and yet be continually content with what we cannot see.

Prayer

Hey Jesus, thank You for calling us out so that You can call us forth. We no longer desire mud pies when we can have a holiday at the sea. Help us be people of great content-ment, not because we like what we see here but because we crave what we can't yet see. In Jesus' name,

* C. S. Lewis, *The Weight of Glory and Other Addresses* (New York: HarperCollins, 2001), p. 26.

AMEN.

Never a Dull Moment

**Your life would be brighter than noonday;
darkness would be like the morning.**

JOB 11:17 NASB

When something is "dull," it usually means
that it has lost some of its light or power—that
is, its life. The substance inside it is running out,
the purpose by which it was created seems to be
lessening, or its existence feels boring or no longer
needed. However, a knife does not get thrown out
when it becomes dull; it gets sharpened so that its original state can be restored.

Now we must ask ourselves: Do our lives feel dull? Does radiating
Jesus feel like a far-off reality? The good news for us is that no matter
where we are and how we arrived there, God can always get us to where
He wants us to go. We are never in jeopardy of losing our identity in Him;
however, we are often in danger of forgetting it. How we define who we
are and what our purpose is will always direct what we radiate to a hungry,
hopeless, and heartbroken world that desperately needs the healing power
of Jesus.

Reflecting on our thoughts, our normal routines, and the ways we spend
our time is necessary. It allows us to evaluate what needs to be added or
removed so that we may run after Jesus, receive His love, and reflect His
light. Our "dullness" is never because we are actually dull in how we were
created; it just means that we need to sharpen our awareness of who we
are in God. As we let Him refine how we see ourselves, we can better reflect
Him. The purpose and promise of our lives have been sealed, but it is our
proximity to our Creator that will determine whether we live them out.

The beautiful thing about being a child of God is that His grace continually reflects through us, even on our hardest days. Our messes radiate His mercy, our struggles reflect His sovereignty, and our hardships point to His healing power. As we work out our salvation, we are able to recognize His fingerprints more quickly and trust Him when life doesn't go our way.

May we take heart when life feels dull, we feel aimless, or situations feel uncertain. Because we know this: Our identity in Him is certain, and because His light penetrates even the thickest darkness, we are never without light. There is never a dull moment when we are walking with the One who placed the stars—what a gift that is.

Prayer

Hey Jesus, thank You for using both my imperfections and my gifts to reflect You. When things feel dull or I'm struggling to understand my purpose, remind me of my identity. You use everything, and Your refinement in me is Your love in action. In Jesus' name,

AMEN.

He never got caught
up in the performance
trap because He was called
to a life of service, not success.
Jesus was not in need of people's
approval, which meant He was
always able to pursue the purpose
for which He was sent.

CHARLOTTE GAMBILL

LIVE YOUR FAITH

Dear Friend,

This book was prayerfully crafted with you, the reader, in mind. Every word, every sentence, every page was thoughtfully written, designed, and packaged to encourage you—right where you are this very moment. At DaySpring, our vision is to see every person experience the life-changing message of God's love. So, as we worked through rough drafts, design changes, edits, and details, we prayed for you to deeply experience His unfailing love, indescribable peace, and pure joy. It is our sincere hope that through these Truth-filled pages your heart will be blessed, knowing that God cares about you—your desires and disappointments, your challenges and dreams.

He knows. He cares. He loves you unconditionally.

BLESSINGS!
THE DAYSPRING BOOK TEAM

———

Additional copies of this book and
other DaySpring titles can be purchased
at fine retailers everywhere.
Order online at <u>dayspring.com</u>
or
by phone at 1-877-751-4347